Mike Tearson

WITH GOD
ON THE FRONTIERS

Scripture Union

130 City Road, London EC1V 2NJ

To Sarah Louise

By the same author:

Devil's Island (with Jimmy Murphy)

Martin Luther: The Man who Lived in Fear

Youth in the City: The Church's Response to the Challenge of Youth Work (with Pete Stow)

© 1988 Mike Fearon

First published 1988

ISBN 0 86201 504 9

Printed and bound in Great Britain by
Cox & Wyman Ltd, Reading

Contents

Foreword

Ninety per cent of young people in the United Kingdom are outside the church and have little meaningful contact with it. Few Christian workers will dare cross the frontiers and meet them where they are. Who then will make contact, build relationships, meet needs, touch their pain, feel their aggression and demonstrate the Good News of Jesus incarnationally?

Nine examples of such individuals come to life on these pages. I note people with strong emotion, character, concern and cultural influence. Here they are with their own wants, flaws, hardships, skills and awareness doing a thankless job. They, the Frontier Youth Workers, often receive the abuse from street kids on one side and 'Why don't these kids come to Church' from Church people on the other.

This work is tackled not because of the status and glory. Not because of the success stories. Not because they love the long, unsocial hours of stretched emotions. This work is tackled, you will read nine times, because there is love – genuine, passionate, all-giving love which will hurt alongside those who hurt and weep with those who weep.

Such love calls people outside their own 'comfort boundaries'. It is only something supernatural that can enable us step outside those areas in which we naturally stay and can confidently move into the uncomfortable zones of life.

Read with your defences down and you will see that 'love rules O.K. ' on these Frontiers.

> It isn't a bell until it's rung
> It isn't a song until it's sung
> It isn't love until it's given away

Pip Wilson
18th July, 1988

Preface

This book is about nine dangerous people.

They are all Christians, though none of them is religious. None are well-known evangelical spokesmen, yet they have more to say that could affect tomorrow's church than a convention platform of famous names. All could be called youth workers, though their roles differ, both from each other's, and from the traditional idea of the work which takes place with young people in church halls up and down the country.

These people have a concern for the young people of our cities, towns and villages – youngsters who are often at odds with society and with themselves – that is costly and sometimes uncomfortable to read about. Theirs is a depth of commitment that puts most of us to shame.

This book is dangerous. It won't make you feel super-spiritual. Its street-level studies of these nine people's work may disturb, challenge or upset. Emulating any of the projects on which they work could make demands on your life, and make you unpopular in your church and community. Taking up the cross of the frontier youth work that they exemplify could lead to a revival in our land – but of a kind that would give most of our churches a bit of a fright!

If you are a young person, you will meet some new friends in these pages. If you are a youth leader, you may find hope, encouragement, some new ideas or a renewed vision, waiting in each chapter. If you are in neither category, perhaps the situations, the atmosphere, the driving beat of the street, and the winners and losers that you will meet will whet your appetite None of the stories is unique; many of them are being re-enacted, probably within a few miles of you, as you read this. There is another chapter or two, waiting to be written. One of them might be yours.

A word of warning. Don't try to read this book in one sitting. These nine are energetic people; they don't let up for a minute and their exploits could run you ragged. Try a couple of chapters at a time. If you have any questions, talk to God about them; a spoonful of prayer will help the stories go down a treat . . .

A word of thanks: to Michael Eastman at Frontier Youth Trust for the seed, John Grayston at Scripture Union for the soil, Bernie, Margaret and Maurice for the beds, the FYT field staff for the wind, nine dangerous people for the refreshing rain, and God for his precious son. They all helped to ease the book through its own growing pains.

The names of the young people have been changed to protect their innocence. The author alone is guilty for any errors that have crept in, though the views expressed by the workers are not necessarily his own.

Here endeth the boring bit. The journey is about to begin; please fasten your seat-belts. . .

Mike Fearon
London, November, 1987

1

On the front line

Noel Hunter – Belfast

Forty young people arriving on the first night of a new youth outreach venture would be a dream come true for most church youth leaders; but Noel Hunter and his colleagues had their reservations.

It was not that the forty all belonged to a local skinhead gang that worried them so much, the night they arrived at the club in the Falls of Belfast. It was the fact that they all came through the door at once – with the police on their tails.

'There was a noise like thunder as they stormed up the stairs,' Noel recalls. 'They'd been down on the peace line, fighting the Catholics!'

The 'peace line' divides the two communities of Belfast. Now a Berlin wall of concrete, twenty feet high with railings along the top, at that time it was simply a no-go area of corrugated iron and barbed wire where fighting was apt to break out at any moment. Members of the Royal Ulster Constabulary, passing in a Landrover, had seen the skinhead gang and given chase.

Noel and his colleagues had just opened up their club in an old mission hall which their church owned. It was a 100-year-old two-storey building in dilapidated condition, standing by itself in the middle of a demolition zone at the very heart of the sectarian fighting. There were no windows on the ground floor, and the walls were covered in graffiti.

It was literally the only building still standing within a quarter mile radius: the only place to which the skinhead gang, caught in the open, could flee. The police drove on past, leaving Noel and the other volunteer helpers to develop a rapport with their new members!

Seven years later, two of those skinheads – now in their twenties – are still regular members. There have been times when it looked as though situations would get out of control, but Noel says confidently that he has never felt in any real danger – even when confronted by some of the toughest lads in Belfast.

The roughness and tension in the area stand in stark contrast to the part of Belfast where Noel spent his childhood. He describes it as 'a nicer area, with working-class terraces of houses with two up, two down and a bit out the back, and where many people had a church connection.'

Noel came to faith in Christ as a boy, through the work of a schoolteacher and a local mission hall, and his faith was nurtured through youth organizations such as the Boys' Brigade. Then the family moved to a local Presbyterian church and Noel started to become involved with voluntary youth work, while working full-time as a teacher. Working his way up through the ranks, he found himself on the club committee before becoming the overall leader.

Around the time that Noel married, he moved to another Presbyterian church – West Kirk, in the rough Shankhill Road area – and began to work as a helper with the youth club for the young people of that church, in addition to his full-time job as a school teacher. The work was unsatisfying, though, because of the common problems of running a club on church premises not specifically dedicated to youth activities: 'You have to set up your club equipment each evening, and take it all down again at the end. It's so frustrating.'

'Some of the young people who were starting to come to the club were not the sort of young folk that some of the church members wanted to see on the premises. They were afraid that something would get broken, or that the place would get soiled.'

In 198(, after Noel and his colleagues had been coping with these difficulties for some years, the Presbyterian denominational youth board decided that each congregation should be encouraged to give some input to an event called Youth Reach. This was a major outreach effort, designed to enable churches to make an impact in their local communities, 'instead of being white elephants'. There were no strict guidelines.

Noel's church decided that they would run a one-week youth mission. 'But the same old problem came up. Where were we going to hold it? Would we go back to the same old ways of doing things afterwards? If we did, it would be great for a week – then we'd have to take everything down for the weekly programme of church activities, and all the young people we'd brought in would split! It would be frustrating, but experience indicated that they wouldn't come back when the place reverted to its usual drab appearance.'

It was at the planning stage that someone suggested using the old mission hall which the church owned. Standing in the middle of a demolition zone in Conway Street, close to the Falls Road district, it had survived only because the church had refused the derisory compensation that the developers were prepared to pay to buy it for demolition.

Forty or fifty people from the West Kirk church

cleaned and painted the building; in fact, on the night the mission began, the paint on the front door was still wet. The young people, mainly from violent street gangs, poured in. It was really just a place for them to go, with a small amount of drama and audio-visuals, and plenty of opportunity for talk and discussion.

When the mission ended, the young people asked if they could come the following week. Noel and his colleagues realised that it would be foolish to stop when they had made so much headway, so pool tables and table-tennis facilities were introduced and the project continued as an open youth club. They called it simply the Centre. A core of about a dozen voluntary helpers who take it in turns to work on the three nights that the club opens have kept the project running ever since.

Sunday nights have always been outreach nights when the activities include a specifically Christian message. It tends to attract heckling and general lack of interest, but over the years some of the young people have responded to the gospel and become Christians. Nevertheless the total number of converts can be counted on two hands.

The other nights are solely recreational. An epilogue isn't felt too advisable on those nights – some young people might take it as a cue to leave the club early.

Young converts with this kind of background have many problems. An added one is to break down preconceptions amongst their peers. 'Bobby, you're a Christian, do you still smoke?' someone asked one night. A nod from Bobby taught the valuable lesson that following God is not about giving things up.

Patrick, a big skinhead, came into the club one night and talked about how he had become a Christian. Within weeks, he was going to church in a suit, with a guitar, a big leather Bible, and a newly acquired Christian girl-friend. Sadly, he had been not only converted, but proselytized. He had abandoned his own cultural background, and the opportunity to relate his faith to others in the situation from which he had come, in favour of the safer route – conformity.

In an environment where broken homes and alcoholism abound, many of the young people live with grandparents because their parents are divorced. Children as young as five or six can be found roaming the streets on a wet night; under-age drinking is common and solvent abuse rampant.

'In the early days,' says Noel, 'gangs of skinheads would come in stoned or "loopy", covered in brick-dust from derelict property where they'd gone to sniff glue. We never had any violence from them, because the solvent intoxification made *any* kind of co-ordinated action impossible. One member managed the impossible, though, one night, in an alley just across from the Centre; he was lying on the ground, high on solvent, hurling bricks at everyone who emerged!'

Patrick recalls, one night while he was still sniffing glue, being stoned in that same alley and looking across to the Centre. It was, he said, surrounded by angels. 'Perhaps he was just hallucinating,' comments Noel, 'but then I read in the Bible about Elisha being protected by chariots of fire. It makes you wonder . . .'

At another club one night, where Noel had been invited to speak, some Christians were singing a song by way of introduction. At the end of the song, they told the assembled young people that 'Jesus can meet all your needs.'

'Will he get me a job?' shouted one comedian in the audience.

The humour was obvious, but there was pain, too, in the remark. Ivor Mitchell, the leader of the club where Noel works, has been able to obtain employment for several of the members, and to find places for others on work schemes at the YMCA where he himself is employed. It is a practical way in which a Christian can show faith to be of practical relevance to these embittered young people.

The sectarian problem is never far away. There are no Catholics in Ivor and Noel's club; it would be too threatening for them. The Belfast YMCA tried to run a non-sectarian club in the city centre, at a time when young people only ever came into the city in gangs, to fight. At times, there were pitched battles, with pool balls flying down the corridor.

Organizations like the Belfast YMCA and Corrymela – a group dedicated to breaking down the sectarian divide – have been influential in bringing Protestants and Catholics together, and convincing them that it is possible to live together in harmony.

At a local drop-in centre, Baptists and Presbyterians work together evangelizing the Catholics; but – because they are not trying to attract them to any particular denomination – it does not create much tension. A Catholic who discovered a renewed faith would probably stay within the Catholic church.

Some Protestant boys have Catholic girl-friends. Others, sadly, gravitate towards political activists and members of paramilitary organizations, finding themselves drawn deeper into a dangerous web.

Members of paramilitary organisations sometimes approach young people in local pubs, typically asking for someone by name, and asking them to do 'a job'. The 'job' might involve transporting a piece of equipment, or carrying a message. From then on, there are subscriptions to pay and meetings to attend. If the young person wishes to withdraw, it becomes extremely difficult. At times like these, the club becomes a refuge for those wanting to stay out of trouble.

There have been evenings when Noel has seen a club member come in looking nervous and fidgety. Then there will be a knock at the door and a figure will appear in the doorway asking for him by name. It is like a page from a corny thriller, but for those who get ensnared, it is far from cliché. 'There are certain boys from the club whom we've had to get out of the country,' Noel says candidly.

Yet, for all the undercurrents of unrest, Belfast is very different from the selective glimpses seen on TV news bulletins. Its most staggering feature is its total ordinariness.

'At one stage, this would have been a very mixed area,' says Frontier Youth Trust staff member Maurice Kinkead, driving through a part of the Falls Road district. 'But, during the early troubles, which flared up in the late sixties, whoever was in the majority would have *burned the rest out* – literally.' It looks like any street in any northern provincial town.

'You wouldn't wander about this area at night on your own; but then, there are parts of most British cities where you wouldn't wander at night by yourself,' Maurice says. As if to illustrate the point, a passer-by suddenly dodged an object that had been thrown at him from a nearby tenement block. There were no soldiers about. This is an area where they only go well protected – in an armoured car, for example – otherwise they would probably be fired upon. Yet it looks like a perfectly normal inner-city neighbourhood. The Centre is only a couple of blocks away.

At one time, the housing situation in the area was chronic, with many people living in decaying houses with outside toilets, rats in the yard, and drains blocked. Re-development has alleviated the worst of the housing crisis, but a hopeless cloud of powerlessness remains.

The feelings of powerlessness and oppression which characterize 'frontier', or pioneering youth situations the UK over are as common in Belfast as elsewhere. Typically, the young people express their pain at being made to wait for hours at the dole office, or at being stopped by the police: 'The police got me, just because I was driving with no licence or insurance,' they say, always feeling hard done by, even when they are in the wrong. Though with widespread unemployment, few can afford to run a car legally.

The Centre receives financial support from West Kirk church, though, as most clubs find, the support has been uneven. There was talk, at one time, of demolishing the Centre and constructing a purpose-built youth centre next to the church building. This was rejected, since the Centre is in a fairly neutral area where the members do not feel intimidated by the proximity of any church building.

Staying in their present location enabled the Centre to obtain a grant from the Education and Library Board to improve the premises. This meant that the club had to close down for a while, to enable the improvements to be carried out. Some of the members started attending other clubs; it was difficult to attract them back.

Winter 1986–87 was spent without adequate heating, because money was scarce. Since then, a gift of £2,500 from a generous church member has enabled a brand new heating system to be installed. Many church members faithfully support the work in prayer. Some make donations towards the running costs, but a minority see it as a waste of resources.

There is little integration between the church and the club. 'From the beginning it was always envisaged that the Centre would not be just for the un-churched, but that the children of church members would be able to use it too,' says Noel. 'In practice, the only Christian young people who come tend to be the children of those who are strongly committed to the work.'

Noel remembers a time when club-members were keen to go to church. 'They went because they wanted to find out what it was like. Once they found out which church was running the club, they would turn up the next Sunday. Sadly, this generated great stress at times.

'I arrived at the church door one Sunday to be greeted by a church leader saying "There's six of them in there, sitting up at the front! You'd better get in there and do something about it!" They were sitting there, fidgetting about, so another club helper and I went up to join them. The service had hardly begun before they started looking at the walls and talking to one another. Being right at the front didn't help; their lack of interest in the worship was transparent to all. One lad came in late, walked down the aisle, looked up at the preacher and went to sit down. I was sweating blood!

'One night, on a pastoral visit, an old lady confronted me accusingly: "There was a boy in church last night, eating chips!"

I said, "Oh, is it worse to eat chips than to eat sweets?" Some older ladies are notorious for sucking sweets during the sermon! I could set my watch by when the polo mints would come out in the choir stalls.'

The situation came to a head one night, in the church porch, when a member of the congregation came out and said, 'Why are that rabble in church?' The young visitors were accused of dragging down the tone of the church, and destroying the atmosphere of worship. Sadly, the young people from the Centre no longer attend, though Noel feels that there is a real desire in the club members to worship. He hopes to set up some form of alternative worship, more suited to their needs.

One night near Christmas, club members experimented with guitar, drums and keyboard, playing Christmas carols to a rock and roll beat. The makeshift band decided to start with a song that the young people would all know, and settled on the refrain 'Here we go', as sung on football terraces the UK over.

That particular night, they had a visit from a couple of local Christians who wanted to see how Noel and his colleagues related to the young people. They were unable to cope with the idea of anyone starting worship with a rousing version of a football song, and left sooner than expected!

Noel and his wife have three children of their own: a girl of seven, and two boys aged nine and three. 'It's a bit painful when the young one comes up to me as I'm leaving for the club, says "Where are you going, Daddy?" and clearly would rather I spent some time with him. My wife is very understanding, and very supportive, though it sometimes generates some tension when I have to concentrate on club-related matters, at the cost of spending time with the family.

Noel feels that he needs to be a part of certain formal church structures in order to maintain a flow of money and good will to the club. 'I find that I *have* to be involved with these other things in order to best represent the interests of the club,' he says. 'It wouldn't be right to neglect those opportunities. It is stressful, though, when we get a run of late nights. Sometimes the police are down at the club till midnight because someone threw a bottle at a P.C. or something. But, thankfully, those times are rare.'

The club has a very poor relationship with the police. On one occasion, they wanted to enter the club to look for people they believed had thrown bricks at a foot patrol. Noel was convinced that the officers would have picked up anyone who vaguely fitted the descriptions, so he denied them entry. Though the police have asserted that the Centre is a harbouring place for bad characters, Noel diplomatically points out that he is trying to keep the young people off the streets, in order to save the police from having to sort out problems on the outside.

Once, when they were trying to set up a community policing scheme, two P.C.'s were allowed into the club; but the tension of having two uniformed officers carrying firearms on the club premises was sufficient to make any repetition undesirable. 'The young people *hate* the security forces,' Noel observes.

In addition to sectarian conflict, solvent abuse and unemployment, promiscuity is common in the Falls Road area. Unmarried mothers often bring their babies into the club.

'I can think of at least six under-25's with children. Some go out wilfully to have a child, because it opens the door to maternity and other benefits, and a place at the top of the council's housing list. The injustice is that a fellow and a girl who want to get married and save up for it stay down at the bottom of the housing list. It pays off to do what is wrong.'

Not doing wrong is a major lesson that Noel has learnt in his years as a voluntary youth worker: 'A worker should try never to succumb to the temptation to tell a lie in a tight situation. If you make a promise, you should always try to keep it. I try to be fair. The young

19

people have to have a high proportion of and a major claim upon a youth worker's time. If the young person knows that a youth worker can be relied upon in small matters, then he/she will more readily accept what the worker has to say about Christianity. You have to build up trust, and that trust is extremely fragile.'

Relationships between churches and their youth projects can sometimes be very fragile, too. It is not just young people who feel growing pains; adults, too are susceptible to the pain that comes with change. It is a costly business, in terms of time, effort and stamina, to be a voluntary youth worker; but it is costly, too, to decide to be a church committed to reaching out to young people in a frontier situation. Buildings may get damaged, the church programme may need to change to accommodate the needs of 'street kids', there is the risk of theft and vandalism, and some people may get hurt.

Jesus knows all about pain, cost and hurt. He never promises that following him would be easy.

2

In the melting pot

Maureen Davies – London

'If there is trouble, you have got to get right in there,' says Maureen Davies, recalling the night two young men pushed past her chasing another lad at the youth club where she was working. 'Chasing after them, I rounded a corner to find the first lad on the floor with the other two kicking him, and holding a knife over him. In my best teacher's voice, I snapped 'Put that knife away,' and then ran forward to help.

'With my hair flying, and a big black leather jacket, I quite shocked them. I do body-building, so I'm fairly hefty! At first, they didn't know if it was a man or a woman coming at them. Then they saw my face as I grabbed and pulled them. One of the lads looked quite stunned when he realized that it was a woman who had done that to him. A *black* woman, too!' she laughs.

'The victim had a blood clot on his brain, but he survived and even came back to the club to thank me for saving his life. That was a big thing for him, because of his attitude towards blacks and women: he thought that women have their uses, but you don't touch blacks unless you have to.

'I don't mind raw racism, and I don't mind the lads being sexist towards me, because you can *see* it – it's out in the open. It's the people who keep their racism, and their sexism, behind those nice, white, lace curtains that I can't stand.

'For me, violence is a part of ordinary life. I'm used to it being around me, and – though it frightens me – I can react to it calmly. A kid will hurt you physically, but you have a chance to defend yourself. A professional worker has more effective, more vindictive, ways to damage you professionally if they want to; and, again, that's behind the lace curtains where you can't get at it.'

Maureen calls herself a celtic black. Her mother is Scottish with Irish descent, and her father is African with Welsh descent. She was born before her parents were married, grew up in Moss Side with pimps, pushers and prostitutes, and her family split up when she was twelve. The origins of her youth work career go right back to being a Sunday school teacher at a small evangelical church in Manchester, in her early teens.

Since then, Maureen has held a long succession of jobs, exploring a considerable number of different aspects of youth work. She began as a school ancillary and a nursery nurse, before working for the Manchester Education Committee and Police Authority on a joint summer playscheme, at the same time doing voluntary work with a uniformed organization called the Campaigners.

The playscheme originated as a response to the early Moss Side rioting which itself followed the Toxteth riot. It was run from a local secondary school, with Policemen in their everyday clothing acting as instructors. Each instructor was involved in a subject which he or she enjoyed, which made them more involved and committed. The response was so good that the project was repeated the following year.

'I spoke to a white boy who was one of the chief organisers of the Moss Side rioting, trying to talk him through the issues involved. I tried to convince him that he would have done better to put his case through the media, instead of through rioting.

'He explained that he had felt very antagonistic towards changes in police policy which had resulted in a lot of officers being moved into Moss Side, because they were moving onto his gang's 'turf', or area of operation. When they found that the police were living in certain, densely black-populated streets, they went around breaking up their homes. Manchester has a long history of racial integration, so black and white kids were supporting each other, because they knew that the heavy policing would be advantageous to neither black nor white gangs. They latched onto the Toxteth riot, and used the same means to make a stand against the police.'

At Westhill college, where she studied for a Youth and Community Work Diploma, Maureen chose to carry out one of her course placements at a lock-up unit – a Secure Home that had once been a Borstal. Located in the rural countryside near Kidderminster, the home contained young adults who were only slightly younger than Maureen herself, and who had been raised in large cities such as Birmingham and Wolverhampton.

'The kids were able to run away at night, but they would get four miles down the road and it would be pitch black, because we were way out in the fields. They couldn't make out where they were going, so they'd have to come back again! If they didn't come back of their own accord, they would be brought back by the police, and their socks and shoes would be confiscated to deter any further escape attempts. I felt that, if I had been tucked up in a place like that, *I'd* want to run away . . .

'Once, when I was on my way back to college, I opened the door of a train compartment and saw these two kids sitting there who had run away a couple of days previously. I sat down with them and said, 'It will take me three minutes to get from here to a telephone. In that time, you can do what you like. You can try to get away, but you have only got three minutes!' I made the phone call, but the lads got away and made it down to London. I thought that was fantastic – it showed great initiative and ability.'

Maureen was the only unmarried woman working at the unit. That, together with the narrow age difference between Maureen and the lads in her charge made it difficult for the young people to work through the sexual, social and racial implications of her being there.

One lad had been a member of the National Front, which might have been a daunting prospect for a black worker, but Maureen was able to work with him in a supportive manner.

The main disadvantage of having so many offenders under one roof, who had been involved in all manner of theft and petty crime, was the way that they were able to pick up tips from each other.

'Because I was a front-line street kid and came from the same type of background, I could understand how they operated. By that I mean they made a point of being very distant, not introducing themselves, sussing people out, and telling all their "hard", stories. Once they had you placed on a scale somewhere between soft and hard, they would test you out, by setting up a situation to see how you would react. Because I was a student, they might have expected me to react one way; and, because I'm a woman, to react in another. I think that I started out "soft" in their estimation, but, by the stories that I told and by the way I reacted to situations, I got to be pretty "hard"!' she laughs.

For her other college placement, because of her background as a nursery nurse, Maureen was assigned to a medical practice in Birmingham, where whe worked with expectant mothers and toddlers. The practice had established an organization called the Larches Green Parosi Group (parosi is the Asian word for 'neighbourhood') which was intended to serve as a community base in a racially mixed area. In addition to the doctors' surgery, the facilities included premises for a playgroup, and a renovated pub which had been converted into a community centre.

Unfortunately, the town planners had struck! A main road had been driven through the heart of the community, which effectively segregated the blacks from the whites. 'I was the only African black person there, working in two different communities and trying to unite them. As soon as the council started refusing our requests for amenities, the Asian community were stumped through lack of knowledge of how the system worked. Because the whites had more knowledge of the system, it became a white person's fight.'

'I encourage black people to get involved with the system, to make it work for them. It doesn't matter where you come from or where you're going; all that matters is who you are. We are not teaching that to young black people, but they are finding it out for themselves. A lot of them are becoming black yuppies and aligning themselves with the Western way, because they cannot cope with the anti-racist work that a lot of black people are doing.

'Black is very much in vogue right now, in the late eighties. It is very vogue to have a black partner. For blacks, having a white partner is a way of being less black, and it makes it easier for them to attain the status they crave. A lot of fashion magazines show mixed partners; suddenly, black is attractive. The black man used to be fashion-conscious to boost his ego, but it is changing. There are now English-sounding blacks as well as ethnic-sounding blacks, and I believe that a new middle-class is emerging. Though it shows how well blacks have moved into, and are using, the system, it is at the cost of their black culture. Black people are becoming *assimilated* to white people.'

But, if many blacks are succeeding in making the colour of their skin irrelevant, others are still feeling the oppression it brings – particularly black women: 'A black guy in Camden once said to me, "Black men are at the bottom of the barrel," and I said, "But black *women* are the ground upon which the barrel is stood. They are even lower down the pecking order." Black women should not have to rise to the male expectations of competition. Traditionally, women from the Third World have had to be independent of their men, because most of them were taken away. Instead of worrying about who we are going to live up to, we can set our own standards. Instead of being frightened of anyone, we can stand fearless. What more can people do to us? When you are at the bottom, there is nowhere to go but up.'

When Maureen ran a playgroup for local children, the white children clearly disliked the involvement of the Asian children, but – with a black women in charge – it was difficult for them to express their racism out in the open. She was able to confront them with their attitudes. If a white lad said, 'Oh, those Pakis stink,' she would turn round and say, 'What do you *mean* by that? What's the difference between calling them Paki and me nigger?' They would say, 'But you're not a nigger, you're Maureen!' Her presence helped to break down the steroptypes, and enabled the white children to see people of other races as rounded individuals in their own right. It is often a lack of understanding of ethnic cultures that causes the uninformed to group individuals together on the basis of their colour: 'Ignorance, fear and history,' says Maureen, 'still play a large part in the way people from other countries are perceived.'

Roots are important to blacks, though to second and third generation British black people, they are becoming less important. Culture is important to everyone, and when it becomes eroded confusion often results: 'I remember being called a monkey by a young black boy. He couldn't relate to my being a black person in a profession. That took me out of my community and away from my culture, in his eyes, and he couldn't cope with that. I tried to explain to him that you don't have to step right outside your culture to achieve status; and that, having achieved status, you become a role model for other black people. Colour is only important to black people in this country because it is *made* to be important. If they were in their native West Indies, professional qualifications would be the most important attribute.'

After successfully completing her college course, Maureen moved to London to work for the Rainer Foundation at a girls' hostel. The project's aim was to provide accommodation for young women who had been in children's homes, and to enable them – after a year or two – to move on into accommodation of their own. 'They were in transit, at an age where they were finding out what it is like to be a woman. They suddenly had more freedom that they had ever known before. They didn't "have problems" but, often, other people created problems *for* them. The demands that teenagers make are not taken seriously; nor are they given credit for knowing what they want to do with their lives.'

Nancy, one of the girls at the hostel, was a glue-sniffer who wanted to return to her mother, but was a ward of court and too young to be allowed to decide where to live. Cindy wanted to go to live with her boyfriend, but couldn't because she had been 'sectioned' – her place of residence had been decided by a court. The local authority social workers considered that both were too young to possibly know their own minds, but Maureen believed that they should be given an opportunity to live their own lives, and a chance to change.

'Working with Nancy, I showed her how I felt, and built up a relationship with her. I saw her at her worst – as a glue-sniffer – and also as a confused little girl trying to grow up. For her, sniffing glue was as much a rite of passage into adulthood as smoking a cigarette had been for previous generations. But the little girl that she still was needed to be cuddled and loved.

'All the young people with whom I work, be they five or twenty-five, I treat as though they were my own child. Treating both Nancy and Cindy in that way, I was able to get quite close to them. It took a lot of work, but I was able to help each to get what they wanted. They were happier for that, because they could live by the decisions that they had made. Just as she was leaving, Nancy turned to me, put her arms around me, and said "Thank you, very much". That said everything.'

It may have been morally suspect for Cindy to have gone to live with her boyfriend, but Maureen sees her job as helping people to get what they want and need, without making any sanctimonious moral judgements: 'Other people's lives are their own. Young people make mistakes; but we all do. Regardless of the quality of life that they will have, they have the *right* – at eighteen – to make their own decisions. I was not going to take the decision away from them, or allow anyone else to take it for them.'

After her period with the Rainer Foundation, Maureen spent some time as a Child Minder Development Officer at Brent, working with older women and single fathers, before working briefly in the USA with black children. 'Kids in the states are *so* advanced compared with kids in this country. Personality-wise, they are far more outgoing – they have really got life sussed out. They are much more street-wise too, but they live in a society where they have to be that way.'

Her next stop was at a day nursery, which she ran for a year: 'A lot of single parents there found that they couldn't pay the fees *and* buy their children shoes. Some yuppies who brought their children there thought that, because *they* could afford to do both, so should everyone else. What angered me was that these yuppies could have afforded to send their children to a private nursery, but were bringing them to the local authority one – taking up places that other people in the local community desperately needed – and were making snide comments.'

Several months were spent running a cafe in Camden, selling good-quality hot food, cheaply. Many local unemployed young people frequented the cafe, and Maureen allowed people who could not afford to pay on the day to pay later, when their DHSS giros arrived: 'I was ripped off three times, but always by people who were working, and could have afforded to pay. Those who were genuinely poor always paid up in the end.'

The range of work that Maureen has tackled comes partly from a desire to find where she fitted in – though she has always stayed with jobs for several months, or years. It is also a reflection of her desire to gain a wide range of work experience. She is not overly concerned with the concept of 'having a career', but, in all her employment situations, she has found ways of expanding her basic brief to enable her to help young people in every way that she can.

'Historically, I grew up with the idea that you don't get "owt for nowt". In my working-class childhood environment, the attitude prevailed that if you had no work, you went and found some. It didn't matter what the work was, but you always found a way of earning a living. I need to earn money, so I've always taken whatever work comes along – and been happy with it.'

At the beginning of 1983, Maureen began to work as a volunteer at the Club House, close to the British Telecom tower, in London's West End. This is a youth and community centre set up by All Souls, Langham Place as part of their urban mission. Concurrent with her nursery job, and then with her stint in the Camden cafe, she fitted in hours wherever she could, typically working one paid evening and one voluntary evening per week – sometimes with the under-10s, but mainly with the senior club. All the normal adolescent problems were there: boyfriends, smoking, sex, a little bit of God, and a lot of general lethargy. But there was nothing that couldn't be managed. Even when one lad came in brandishing a machette, it could be handled!

'His name was Jimmy, and he was black kid. A couple of other black kids in the club had been threatening him, so he came in tooled up to sort them out.

Colin Chapman, the Club House leader, reasoned with him. Colin and Jimmy went out, followed by the two lads he had come to see – who were armed with pool cues. I followed them out, and we defused the situation, verbally. It was really very run-of-the-mill. All very dramatic, but what an anti-climax – we just sat and talked.'

The few black young people who attended the Club House suffered growing pains as they approached adulthood because they lacked a positive image of black people. It was a white-dominated environment, even though there was little racial tension. With Maureen and Gary – another black worker at the Club House – as positive role models, the situation became more promising.

The biggest racial problem that Maureen has had to face has been with young people of mixed race. Like Maureen, neither completely black nor completely white, they felt that they did not belong anywhere – and were often made to feel that that was the case: 'I have been told by blacks that I am *useful* to them, but that I an not actually one of them. Trying to "find yourself" in that situation is difficult – *that* growing pain is hard to bear. Two lads of mixed race that I have known have acted violently, but – because of the influence of the Club House – they have grown through the violent stage to become well adjusted young men.'

Maureen found it difficult to establish specific girls' work at the Club House. With her other commitments, she was unable to dedicate the concentrated time that would be required. Also, the male workers were slightly condescending – and sexist! – about the possibility. They had tried it before and it had failed, but Maureen was not one to tolerate such a defeatist attitude.

31

'Poor old St. Paul was trotted out too, by anti-feminist elements in the Club House – without regard to the context in which Paul wrote. But the biggest problem lay in the small number of local girls who attended the Club House. How could we maintain a constructive girls' group with only four girls?' In consequence, much of Maureen's effort to establish girls' work in that situation consisted of combating the arguments against it, and talking with other female workers.

In 1985, she embarked upon another full-time job. The Winchester Project, based in Camden, was set up in 1974, and incorporated a motor-cycle workshop, a general youth club, a black outreach worker, an educational workshop and a sports worker. The motor cycle workshop was used as a basis for intermediate treatment with young people whose special needs required sympathetic attention. There were also two women's workers, who were not specifically called by that title. Maureen was one of those workers. During the two years that she worked there, she encountered not only antagonism towards the work that she was doing, but also a lack of respect towards herself as a person. A battle on the twin fronts of racism and sexism was being waged, not from the outside, but from the inside.

'Our fight was for proper recognition for the work that we were doing with females aged eight to twenty-two. We started at eight on the grounds that a girl can start her menstrual cycle that young. The work covered a cross-section of races and sexual preferences.

'We had two gay young women, Jill and Louise, who were having a hard time coming to terms with their sexuality. I had to accept them as they were, and to build on that platform. As they "came out", it was hard for the other young women who had known them to accept them when they found out.' Maureen had to work through the emotional turmoil, not simply of the two lesbians themselves, but of their friends. She found the turmoil that was expressed to be very similar to that of growing up black, or crippled, or anything that society does not see as 'normal'.

'I told them that I was a practising Christian and, because I knew that God has a plan for their lives, it didn't make any difference that they were gay – just as it wouldn't make any difference whether they were black or white. Other gay women joined the group, which made it easier for Jill and Louise to state where they stood. Reactions from their friends ranged from, "My God! I'll never speak to you again!" to being really understanding. Jill and Louise were able to accept themselves and to combat the repression that they felt.'

Maureen took the women's group motor-cycle scrambling, gliding, and horse-riding, in addition to running discussion groups and organising activity days. With such a broad spectrum of activity available, even the youngest girls were enthralled. In a 'girls only' situation, they were freed from playing up to the lads to the extent that they no longer wanted to have them around all the time. Photography and jewellery-making were added to the programme as numbers grew.

'Isn't it great, just us girls together?' they said, freed from any sexual competition for the boys' attention. 'When a group of lads go down to the pub to have a few beers and talk about football, they have a whale of a time,' says Maureen. 'So do girls in a youth club together. You can talk about period pains, sex and your boyfriend. Men really are a pain in the kneecap; why *should* girls aways have to dress up for them?

'Single-sex work gives young people the opportunity to find out that they are "all right". That if a lad of sixteen is not sleeping around, he is not the only one. Kids today are pretty much together. They have no hang-ups about starting periods, or bodily functions, nor about talking them through. As long as there are others of the same sex around to say, 'It happens to us all,' that is all that they need to hear.'

Maureen feels that adults make problems for young people by pressuring them and denying them the opportunity that they need just to become adults in their own good time and in their own way. The parent, vicar, youth worker, or even the teen magazine can impose upon young people by not standing back and letting them discover things for themselves.

Maureen recalls seeing a girl of ten giving a very sexual 'come-one' to a man of forty. She had been forced to be aware of sexuality by peer group and society pressure.' This wasn't completely negative, however: 'She *needed* to be aware. She needed to know, if a man came up to her in a certain way, that he was making a sexual advance: it could make the difference between being abused and not being abused.'

Young people see the forms of love that adults display and mimic them, though they may constitute a very perverse role model. Maureen remembers, in her late teens, 'going through a Germaine Greer stage, the throw-out-your-deep-freeze-and-in-comes-free-love kind of thing.' It took her a long time to realize that community love and family love were being displaced by a wishy-washy free love that was so nebulous that it meant nothing. Young people in the late eighties are growing up in the aftermath of that. They don't know what love is. A lot of parents are saying, 'You don't need me. Be yourself, be independent,' and today's youth are saying, 'But Mummy, I need you; Daddy, I need you.'

Free love, Maureen says, can be a form of abuse. It can also create expectations which result in abuse. Maureen had to counsel a young person who discovered that. She had been raped. The incident was particularly traumatic because the woman was gay and the man who raped her the brother of a friend. But the details that were presented were so confused, and the girl so out of touch with her own feelings and reactions, that she actually may have been giving powerful 'come-on's' to the man, who may honestly have felt that the victim was consenting. Or, again, he may simply have despised the fact that she was gay.

One of Maureen's colleagues who was working with the rape victim found it difficult to cope with the situation. The colleague was also gay, and was taking on board all the anger that the victim felt about men. Maureen had to support her colleague as well as the girl who had been raped.

'The whole issue of being gay: I wonder, when do you decide that you are? I believe that there are many young people who desperately want to have a relationship with someone, anyone. Being gay is promoted so much by society that some young people choose it, believeing it to be a valid option.

'It was taxing for the other worker, who was caught in a cycle of being alternately rejected and drawn close by the victim. I tried to be an objective outsider, helping the other worker see where she was being overtly subjective. In the end, the worker was able to stand firm and allow the victim the space to sort out her feelings for herself.'

Drink and drug abuse are, Maureen believes, a part of the rebellion of young people growing up. When taking girls' football teams away for a weekend, it was not uncommon for some of the girls to get 'legless' after a match. Smoking pot has been fairly common among the girls with whom she has worked, but hard drugs tended to be frowned upon, particularly by the blacks.

General youth work at the Winchester Project was very different from youth club work at All Souls Club House. The young people were racist and very sexist, with the males pushing the females around and treating them abominably in relationships. 'My first confrontation with a white boy there occured when he threw chairs at me. ' ''Pick them up,'' I said, ''If you want to have a temper tantrum, go home to Mummy, but don't do it with my chairs.'' '

Maureen has seen changes in many of the young people with whom she has worked. Instead of storming off in a huff about some imagined wrong, she has seen them develop the maturity to confront what is going on around them, and to work through the feelings and emotions that are involved. Working with an educationally subnormal girl, Maureen and her colleagues were able to help her towards a level of independence, and to accept that level of independence.

'I've brought young people to Christ in a number of different settings. There is a particular way that I work, and I believe that the Lord leads me to particular people who need someone like me, and the way that I work. Basically, I meet someone who may be associated with other Christians, but who has not him/herself been through a conversion experience. I ask him or her if they are a Christian and, if not, I say ''Why not?'' in my usual forceful way!

'Whatever reasons or reaction I get, I explain why they are not good enough reasons as far as God is concerned. Rather than get people into an emotional frenzy, or zap them with the gospel, I leave them to rationally consider the claims of Christ. I ask them to go away and pray. "Commit your life to Christ, then come back and tell me when you have done it," I say, "Or tell me why you won't accept Christ, but make you decision, and make it on your own."

'I don't think that Christians are sufficiently willing to confront people with the truth. They convert people by emotional pressure, and they quickly fall away. Jesus was not like that. He told James and John to leave their nets and follow him. They could either go with him or refuse his invitation, but he left them with no other option. If you want Christ, you have to take him and not mess him about.'

In Autumn 1987, Maureen joined Frontier Youth Trust as London area Field Officer. 'I have a vision that, with the FYT network, there are enough youth workers to change the face of youth work over the next few years. We're not going to have much money, but praise God for that; when we have God, we have everything. We have to trust him and to work for his kingdom to come to young people. It means finding the right solutions to the right situations.

'I'm going to enjoy enthusing people to get off their backsides. I want to see youth workers being a really professional fighting force, where Christ is concerned. I think that we can do it. Let's go for it.'

3

Let's go down the Shewsy!

John Hutchinson – Liverpool

For twenty years, the church has been struggling to meet the needs of young people in inner-city areas. Yet the outlook for these people appears to be bleak. Does the gospel need to be redefined to make it relevant to today's young people? Or is the Christian faith in the industrial world on an inevitable decline?

These are the sort of questions John Hutchinson is trying to work out answers to in the district of Everton, Liverpool, where he works. Is there still faith in the city? Are Christians to be like Nehemiah, rebuilding the city; or like Lot, nipping out the back door, before the whole show goes up in flames? Standing on John's doorstep, looking out over the bare bones of redevelopment, it looks more like Jericho after Joshua has been.

John's is a classic inner-city situation. Multiple problems have piled on top of each other until something has to give. The frustrations and tensions of the people of the area find their outlet in the form of vandalism, hooliganism, petty crime, a black-market economy and a loss of enthusiasm for living.

'Unemployment, plus bad housing, plus lack of maintenance, plus lack of facilities, equals a real nightmare,' says John. 'On top of that, the planning was disastrous. It's quite incredible that we can't produce town planners who can get it right. The whole business of having families in high-rise blocks doesn't work.'

'For the size of the immediate community, there is a good shopping facility – but it's an unbalanced facility,' adds his wife, Hilary. 'There are *four* butchers shops, which are forever closing down because they cannot compete; but new ones keep coming.' There is a very limited range of goods available; residents have to make the mile-and-a-half journey into the centre of Liverpool for many of their weekly necessities.

The Hutchinsons have shared in the joys and frustrations of the people of Everton for more than sixteen years. John's arrival as a youth worker in the first place, however, was a complete accident. In 1971, having recently left the public school where he was educated and spending some time on a scholarship in America, he was sitting in a country cottage trying to write poems! He moved up to Liverpool to work at a church in Everton, through contact with the vicar. For several weeks he stayed at the Shrewsbury House youth and community centre – the 'Shewsy', as it is affectionately known to the locals.

'After I'd been here for a week, I was running the door at the senior club practically single-handed! That was a shock for a green southerner. Staying at the club introduced me immediately to a lot of practical youth work.

I was delighted. The experience gave *me* as much as I was able to give back.'

At that time, the Shrewsbury House club was housed in an old building on a new estate. An epidemic of tower-block construction had left the estate with nearly two dozen blocks, standing like concrete tombstones in a space that would have been overcrowded with half that number. Beginning in 1957, post-war slum clearance had resulted in a massive redevelopment featuring high-rise flats, maisonettes, low-rise complexes and communal areas, all densely packed together and about as conducive to healthy community life as the local cemetery.

The club was planning a new building for its own accommodation, but wanted to incorporate facilities for the local community, which had started to look on it as a focal point for community affairs. At the same time, the diocese was examining ways of rationalising the churches in the area. These two aims gave birth to a centre which combined a church, a youth club, a hostel, and accommodation for staff – and which was very much at the heart of the community.

It wasn't an overnight transformation. Six or seven years of hard work and planning were required, during which time John met and married Hilary, who had been working part-time at the 'Shewsy'. John had arrived part way through the planning, and was able to contribute some of his own ideas. The new building opened in 1974. 'For a year during the construction we'd been meeting in an old primary school,' John adds.

In 1987, the whole area was in the midst of a second wave of redevelopment. The first had failed, and the town planners had decided to try again. Six tower-blocks were demolished within a year, and six more stood empty, waiting for the hammer to fall. 'It's an extraordinary history of transformation,' says John. 'Over thirty years, the whole area will have completely changed – twice. In consequence, there remains no real community identity. There has been a tremendous breakdown in personal trust. There is complete dislocation in who *lives* where, and what is *placed* where.

That gives rise to a good deal of basic insecurity and uncertainty.'

That is brought home by a brief walk around the estate. At the local off-licence, it is impossible for a customer to directly reach any of the goods on display. Ceiling-high perspex panels intervene between the customers and merchandise. Only the staff – quarantined on the other side – can reach the goods and hand them to the purchaser through a small rectangular slot in the perspex, while a security closed-circuit TV camera looks on. It is like a scene from George Orwell's book, *Nineteen Eighty-Four*.

Outside, the wind howls around the remaining tower blocks with boarded-up faces. Mounds of rubble mark the last resting place of hundreds of homes, and walls of crinkled iron bar the way back to dwellings which have been vacated more recently. There are few people about in the autumn evening, and John muses about the lack of community; 'there's just a collection of people who don't know and don't trust each other – who are not their brother's keeper.'

The current situation has arisen largely out of the politics of the city council – the hard-left governing by confrontation. After the old militants were removed from office for their stand on rate-capping, and for refusing to set a rate, the new more moderate council apparently intended adding more consultation to the process of local government. The council plan is to flatten the area, leaving only Shrewsbury House and a handful of the newer tower blocks, for families without children. It is intended that the Shewsy become a water sports centre serving an artificial lake which will be considered in the middle of what is to become Everton Park.

'The church building has caused the planners a head-

41

ache! They can't get rid of it, yet it's integrated as an essential part of the centre. Possibly the plan will become compromised, anyway, and result in a mix of park and housing. Parks are not too attractive to people in most cases, unless there is some special feature of interest. I wonder if it will receive much use from the nearby residents.' Though the first wave of redevelopment was disastrous, it looks as if the second attempt will be a success.

'The council's programme of urban regeneration is visionary. Whatever the methods, which range from being questionable to downright criminal, the aims have remained intact, and many of them have been achieved. It has upgraded the quality of life for a large number of people. They may have had to move away from where they've lived for the past twenty years, but, as we've seen, there wasn't much of a community life here anyway, and now many people have homes with gardens and their own front door.'

Whatever the merits of the latest redevelopment, one bone of contention is that it was carried out mainly by outside contractors, using little in the way of local labour.

Certain large families used to be power-brokers on the estate; no one wanted to get on the wrong side of them: 'For all our efforts, there was still a no-go mentality, based on the reputations of these families, that we couldn't beat.' But now that no one lives within close proximity to the club, the Shewsy is more neutral; it is safe ground for everyone.

'People wear the problems of the inner-city on their sleeves. The more I think about it, the more I believe that it's an obvious consequence of being shunted about that people smash windows, break doors, find it difficult to attend school for more than one year out of five, and see no prospect of employment. In fact, the only thing which surprises me is the resilience and strength of character that the people display in spite of all that.

'Liverpool is sometimes called "the capital of Ireland", because of the large numbers of Irish immigrants who have made it their home. This area was once part of loyalist Orangeland, but – though nominally still Protestant – it is now populated by an almost entirely Catholic community. In the early '60's, the club was strongly Protestant, and *did not allow Catholics to enter*. But there again there's been a real transformation. That kind of attitude would be unthinkable now.'

Now, Catholics and Protestants are working together on community issues in a tremendous fashion. There has recently been a major battle to save some good houses, against the council's wishes. Militant councillors have been in court, and the local community is asking the housing corporation for £750,000 to do the homes up. For a change, it's not just the Shewsy getting involved, and the mark of it has been some sort of ecumenical co-operation that was unheard of even a decade ago.

The housing upheaval has added to the pains of the area's young people, coping with the difficulties of adolescence and striving towards adulthood. Many families have broken up, and other homes seem threatened with break-up, as the tensions take their toll. John can reel off a list of additional worries which cause pain to the young people in Everton: 'Boring schools and the prospect of desultory jobs; the threat of drugs; living in Everton rather than Dallas; the prospect of not doing anything exciting, other than drinking; not having any money; and getting caught shoplifting.'

In the club one night, a lad expresses his pain at the violence he sees around him. Speaking too quickly and quietly for his thick scouse accent to be easily understood, he tells that he has personally witnessed six muggings within the last few years. Another fifteen-year-old explains that he has not been to school for a year. He prefers to spend his time in a betting shop where, as an under-aged gambler, he is quickly becoming an expert student of racing form.

Though there is little visible violence in the area, as a rule, there has recently been a spate of knife attacks – violence that is drug-related, perhaps someone stealing at knife-point to finance a purchaser, or someone who has not settled up a debt with a drug dealer.

'The problem with knives,' says John, 'is not when you take one out and use it, but when you first put it into your pocket. What are you thinking when you do that? It's an action either born out of fear, or out of a completely uncontrolled approach to other people. We had one eleven-year-old in the club carrying a cut-throat razor the other night; but generally people only get violent when they've been drinking.'

'When we first came here, violent crime was hardly ever heard of,' adds Hilary. 'It was only against businesses, not individuals. It's becoming worse, if the form of muggings.'

John finds in the young people who come to the Shewsy a great fear of going anywhere which appears threatening. The solution is to take as many mates along as possible. Football trips are a classic example: a strange town becomes home turf if it is bombarded with as much Liverpool culture as they can take with them. This unfortunately usually involves everyone getting drunk at the same time!

Regular trips organized by the club are regarded as 'safe' by the local young people: they bear the mark of familiarity. But to try to get them, say, to Greenbelt, is a different matter entirely. It is a strange, and therefore threatening environment to them. Only the bravest will go – the ones who celebrate their own individuality. Another problem with trips is that the girls always feel that they have to take an iron and a hair-dryer with them, even if it is only for one night away!

Dressing smartly is another popular syndrome – to spend a lot more money than they can afford on clothing, to go out looking 'hip' and to laugh at others who are less trendy. It is a way of acquiring self-esteem.

Illegitimate income is regarded as quite acceptable on the estate. There is a high level of theft, receiving stolen goods and shop-lifting. It forms a large part of young people's lives though they do not regard it as serious crime. One of the more unsavoury aspects of this black economy are the several girls who regularly sleep with certain lads, in exchange for money. The money may then, perhaps, be used to purchase heroin, which is not uncommon in the area.

'The area's biggest export is people. They always aspire to move upwards and outwards. Very few young people who acquire particular skills, or who have particular luck in the job market, remain part of this community.'

There is a frequent exodus to the south by small groups of young people, and John considers that there must be thousands of young scousers living on the south coast, where they have gone in search of work.

A standard method of generating income is to sign on the dole in Liverpool, then go down to London and sign on there, too. In London, they apply for an accommodation allowance at a bogus address, tip the house owner a few pounds for the use of the address, and then head back up to Merseyside. There are, however, some young people who find legitimate jobs in the south.

In the estate around the Shewsy, it is the minority who are in employment. The expansion of MSC schemes is the biggest factor in taking local young people out of the dole queues. Among the schemes which the Manpower Services Commission have run in Merseyside in recent years have been a project to catalogue birds' eggs at the local museum, and a scheme to catalogue all the council-owned art treasures. It was as a result of this scheme that a sculpture by an Italian master was located, which had been whitewashed and left in a school quadrangle for years!

The club's work is to identify the needs of young people, and to meet those needs, in order that they can become established as part of the community. The Shewsy aims to be the best youth club in the area. A junior club for 5–12 year-olds is held three times in the week, and a senior club, for 13–21 year-olds five times. It is very activity-orientated: within these clubs are run discos, a wide range of sporting activities, guitar and music lessons, photography, video, a club magazine, and weekends away. Many members, though, are completely lacking in ambition or a desire to widen their experience, and they are content simply to use the premises to shoot a few frames of pool. They just want to 'have a laugh'.

None of the club-users lives in the immediate vicinity of the centre. Many of them have to catch a bus home, and nearly all the members pass at least one closer youth club on their way. Yet the members' loyalty is undiminished. Not only do members who used to live nearby return each club-night, but new members who have never lived nearby, or who were too young to attend when they did, have started to come.

'Different groups are at different stages,' John observed in his official report on the club's work in 1986. 'One young man who recently overturned a crane on a demoliton site leads a group which shuns personal contact as much as possible, but he is in the club every night. We take lots of anger and aggression (and the building takes some damage) and make only tentative steps in forming relationships. The groups of girls, now a majority in the club, are usually delightfully keen to turn their hand to almost anything on offer, and with them, the bonds of relationships are stronger and deeper.

'Not long ago, we organised a sponsored event in the form of an all-night disco-dancing marathon. The occasion was exclusively for girls, and parents' permission had been properly sought and received for all participants. There was some pleading and some anger from the lads but nothing, or so we thought, that we could not handle. At 4.00am on this cold, wet autumn night we discovered four shivering little bodies on top of one another sandwiched into the two-foot space between the outside doors and the roller shutters, huddled in a vain attempt to sleep. All our first thoughts of fury were turned as we uncovered and listened to some of their stories. Streetwise they certainly were, but locked out, partly unloved and going off the rails were also plain truths in their young lives. Clearly there was a need for discipline and respect, but plainer still was their need for security, affection and real care.

'Club activities and material achievements have continued to develop well. The new minibus has been used to the full, a club car has been a short-term but useful feature, enabling senior members to practise driving and basic mechanics. The senior lounge has been put to reasonable use with drama, aerobics, glass-engraving, reading room, and senior member discussion group all being a small part of the programme. The guitar class flourished well, and we have an excellent documentary of the area's transformation recorded on video. In the field of sport, the club team won the Merseyside Youth Association Cricket League and, most notably, the under-19 five-a-side football team became champions of Great Britain after regional and national tournaments.'

One new pressure on the club, which emerged in summer 1987, was the presence of several pubs and clubs in the centre of Liverpool that began to run special discos for the under-18's in the city. Operating on Mondays, Tuesdays and Wednesdays, they were clearly attempting to attract, early on, a clientele that would stay with them until old enough to come to the main weekend discos. John feels that this is an unprincipled move based on exploitation: 'The pubs are completely indiscriminate over who they let inside. They are licensed clubs which, for these special discos, sell only soft drinks, but I doubt if an under-18 would get turned away if they arrived on a main night when alcohol was on sale.' Though admission to these discos costs more than a pound – compared with twenty or thirty pence at a Shewsy disco – going to a 'proper' disco club obviously appeals to the young people's egos and vanity. It's a strong talking-point, and a source of prestige, to tell your school friends that you were at a swanky night-club the previous evening.

John's colleagues include one full-time youth worker, three part-time youth workers, five part-time community workers, a full-time caretaker, part-time cleaning staff, and about twenty voluntary workers. The hostel which forms part of the premises houses Christian young people, mostly post-graduates, gaining life experience in an environment far removed from that to which they are accustomed. They work as volunteers in the club and community. John describes how they arrive feeling threatened and vulnerable, and leave as though they have been through the transforming year of their lives. They throw their arms around everyone and say 'See you again'. It is as if *home* had a meaning for the first time in their lives. Some of them are still coming back to visit ten years later. There has been bridge-building too, with the Shrewsbury public school, who originally founded Shrewsbury House as a mission. Pupils from the school regularly visit Everton on field trips.

Though there may seem to be a lot of staff, and visitors often comment about how well the Shewsy is equipped, it is badly off by comparison with many statutory schemes. With present staffing and funding, it is possible to keep the club 'ticking over', but there are simply not enough man-hours in the day to effectively change the attitudes, and really affect the lives, of young people.

Some of the funding which the project receives is spent on sending part-time workers on local authority training courses. About thirty leaders have gone through the part-time youth worker scheme in the past eight years. Regular helpers' meetings – every three or four weeks – provide opportunities for brainstorming, evaluation, review and planning. Five or six key staff members meet separately, too. All these sessions contain training input. Local and national voluntary umbrella organizations also offer training, which the Shewsy uses as and when it can afford the fees.

There is a strong emphasis on pushing senior members into leadership roles, and the current staff is made up almost entirely of people who have 'graduated' from being regular members. Some, but not all, have become Christians en route. 'Chris Wittington and Peter Brown are two outstanding examples,' says John. 'Chris has never worked in any other field since he first set foot inside the club. He came to help out and, after five or six years, completed a part-time training course, and a full-time two-year youth and community course. Peter, too, has successfully completed the course.'

A small number of young people regularly attend the services at St. Peter's church adjoining the youth club. At one time, congregations of 120 at a service were not unusual, but, with more than 3,000 people moving away in the previous year, numbers are much lower – perhaps fifty in total at a morning service. The challenge to the church has been to transfer the catchment area from the doorstep to something further afield. It has proved easier for the club to make the transition than for the church.

For John Hutchinson, the last few years have been a hard slog; yet he is full of admiration for the 'wonderful local people who stand up to everything that is thrown at them, and create a personal quality of life that has nothing to do with material values. They don't hoard their money; they happily spend it without worrying about it.'

Julian Charley, Rector of St Peter's Church, as well as Warden of Shrewsbury House, concurs with these sentiments. He concluded the 1986 report with these remarks: 'We live here in a world full of rumours. They seem these days to be characterised more by hope than by gloom – and there seem to be some grounds to justify it. Add to that local humour, warmth and resilience, and you have a promising mixture. Someone staying here recently said of the area, 'I've never met such warm-hearted people''. And so say all of us.'

4

Bringing home the bacon

Willy Holland – St Helens

'Kids are realizing that there's a life worth the living,' says Willy Holland. 'They want to get caught up in experiencing Jesus. We are seeing conversions within the club. In a lot of churches and Christian youth clubs, Jesus doesn't come into the picture; the Holy Spirit isn't given a look-in. But when the kids come into contact with a fellowship where he *is* acknowledged, the result is life-transforming. I've taken parties of young people to those churches and the kids have been so excited, they've said, "Are we going again next week?" '

Willy's open youth club is tucked away down a side street in Parr – a suburb of St Helen's, Merseyside. Yet the whole atmosphere of the estate where the club is situated resembles that of an inner-city community, close to the centre of a sprawling metropolis.

The street is 'unadopted', which means that no one claims to own it, or care for it. Until recently, it was little more than a dirt track. Willy has a wry 'bride-wore-wellies' story about a wedding reception that was held at the club on a day when bad weather had turned the road into a river of mud.

The 'Y' Club – officially called St Helens YWCA – faces onto a tarmacked square. As you stand in the centre and turn through 360 degrees, turn-of-the-

51

century terraces give way to post-war council flats, a row of small shops, a block of old people's flats, a strip of wasteland with gasometers behind and, finally, the club itself. The square had been scheduled for redevelopment, but the discovery of an old mineshaft underneath meant that the new supermarket scheme which had been planned had to be abandoned. The square has now been made into a vast car park – ironically, since few people in the area can afford to run cars!

'I'm a local lad,' says Willy. 'I started coming to the club when I was fourteen or fifteen, and kicked it about a bit. I was part of a big gang. We saw ourselves as "rockers" or "Hell's Angels", and this was our base'.

'At that time, the club was run by a Christian – Pip Wilson – who constantly told us all about Jesus and the good things we could have if we followed him. Pip used to present the Gospel to us every day. After a while, we got the idea that we were the "Lions" and he was the "Christian"! A lot of Christian events were put on there, and our job was to "give it some stick".

'As the years passed, Pip began to strike me as being genuine in what he talked about. I began to ask myself, "If he's right about the things he's been saying, where does that leave me?" '

After eight years of being a "Lion", Willy defected to the other side.

'Things began to change. Not overnight, but over a period of months. I eventually saw that I had a part to play in this area, certainly in young people's lives. Because I'm from the area, I could identify with them; I knew some of their needs. I started off by doing voluntary work here. Then Pip left and another full-time worker came in. After a few years, I got married and my wife and I got caught up in voluntary work with young people in our local church. I left the "Y" Club to run the open youth work there.'

The young people at the church took up most of his free time, but Willy kept the 'Y' Club at the back of his mind. Then Linda, his wife, heard that there were difficulties at the 'Y' Club – the full-time worker had left. She began to pray about the situation.

'I had a good job at the local glassworks, but Linda kept saying that I ought to apply for the full-time vacancy at the "Y" Club. I had no qualifications for the job, so I thought the idea was ridiculous. Linda kept on about the idea so, to get her off my back, I applied for the job – not really expecting to get an interview.'

But Willy *was* asked along to the club for an interview. When he arrived, he found that the building somehow felt different: The presence of God and the love of Jesus seemed to be missing. The other people being interviewed were highly qualified, so Willy was confident that he would not be offered the position. It came as something as a shock when he was!

Accepting the job would mean selling their semi-detached house with its own garden, and moving into the dismal, graffiti-scrawled YWCA building. Socially, that would be a step down. But Linda felt strongly that he should accept.

'Then, a few days later, I got wind of redundancies coming up at work.' Willy says poingantly. They began to feel that God was active in the situation and, after a week of prayer, he accepted the job. That was in 1980.

'The first problem that we encountered was glue. The number of glue-sniffers in the area was fantastic.'

The Hollands decided that the solution was to show love to the young addicts and to make them feel wanted, so they opened up their flat – and their lives –

to them. Linda and Willy took them as they were, at *their* level. All that they asked in return was respect.

It began to work. Regularly, they would be woken in the night by people in need of immediate help ringing their doorbell, but they stuck at it. Then they began to answer the door to find no one there; but left on the doorstep would be items that had been stolen from the club years before – items such as microwave ovens and deep-fat friers!

It was as if the young people were saying, 'We know what you're about. We're not going to knock it anymore. We'll respond.' Because the Hollands were giving them something to do and to think about, the young people began to pack in the glue-sniffing. Three of them are now voluntary workers at the club; two have become Christians. 'They were the biggest thieves around here!' Willy remembers. There are many others whose lives have changed, and who are close to making a commitment to Christ.

Willy took a lesson from Pip Wilson and relied heavily on personal contact: 'Pip used to physically greet us every evening with a punch on the shoulder! At that time, I had relished physical contact, and the action was one that acknowledged my toughness. It had made me feel welcome.'

Though Willy occasionally held evangelistic meetings at the 'Y' Club, particularly using loud gospel groups with a 'hard' edge – mostly it was the one-to-one contact that really cut through to people and changed them.

Willy was still the only full-time worker at the club, though he gradually built up the part-time staff till he had six part-time colleagues – paid by the local authority – and four voluntary workers. The club began to run its own in-service training, with a strong input from the YWCA, supplemented by local authority material and material they produced themselves. The mix of staff – then, as now, some Christians and some not – caused no problems, but a lot of challenges. It was exciting.

In 1985, Willy and the other staff began to feel that the club needed to be modernised and expanded. Willy went down to London to talk with the YWCA management, who own the building. The YWCA launched a national appeal and put together plans to transform the building. The cost was estimated at £75,000. The money started to trickle in, and work started in December 1986.

At that time, the club was drawing about fifty young people per night. There was every reason to be encouraged. But financially, the club was struggling.

As the conversion work got under way, the amenities – which for some time had not been able to provide everything that the community needed – were steadily refurbished. New showers, changing rooms, workshops, sports facilities, and provisions for disabled people were the outward signs of modernisation. The club's renewed vision was expressed in an extra evening of youth work and a greater emphasis on adult work.

When the rebuilding work started, early in 1987, Willy spoke of his goals as follows: 'Firstly, we need to seriously look at the adult community and bridge the gaps that exist between young people and their elders. We are looking to set up groups for the unemployed, too.

'Secondly, drug abuse needs to be tackled. The breakdown in family life, reflected in inadequate parental supervision and concern for their children, means that young people are becoming increasingly bored, and increasingly keen – mistakenly – to prove their maturity through drink and drug abuse.

'We've got "speed" and marijuana being used. Solvent sniffing currently centres around *Tipp-Ex* – the typewriter correction fluid. That's more the girls – perhaps because they do typing at school and college. They bring it along, put it in plastic bags, and hide it in toilet system. Once you've had a can of lager with it, it's a cheap way of getting "high".

'Another related problem is the attraction of the local pubs – and even nightclubs – to under-aged drinkers. One or two eighteen-year-olds are aggravating the problem by purchasing cans from off-licences on behalf of those who won't pass for eighteen in the pubs. Re-education, but amongst the older club members and the local licencees, is clearly needed.'

By the end of 1987, as conversion was drawing to a close, the position had changed drastically. The club's financial difficulties had abated: 'There has been a complete change-around. Finance proved to be our biggest head-ache over the year, and the club was threatened with actual closure. But the appeal that was put out in 1985 finally raised more than £100,000, of which £85,000 had to be ploughed into the redevelopment, but the remainder has been invested to cover our on going costs. The local community – while giving very little financially – is queueing up to use the building.

Non-Christians rely on practical things – for them, seeing is believing – but that is very different from our God-centred approach. It's been as if a veil has been lifted. The area's reputation had improved, and it is no longer known as an area of ill repute. Kids are really responding; it's an answer to prayer. God has been faithful to us as we have stepped out in faith.

'We've still got a superb team of youth workers; there is very little conflict – it gells and works together.

Everything is shared. There is a great atmosphere amonst the staff, and it is reflected in the club.

'A year ago, some of the girls were getting really caught up into drink and drugs. Through frequent conversation and discussion, they have been given opportunities to take on active roles in the club; some of them have been on leadership courses. Local folk are taking on responsibility, and there have been fewer attemps to break into the premises.'

While the conversion was taking place, it became impossible for the club to operate within its building. Willy suddenly found that his role had switched to that of a detached youth worker, working with young people without having a building to which he could take them back:

'We operated in the mini bus, taking the kids here, there and everywhere – visits to the park, Blackpool and Southport. We never lost touch with the young people. With only one 15-seater vehicle, a lot of shunting was required. Often 35–40 people wanted to go on a trip, so our team would be forced to make three journeys to cater for the demand.

'Those hard times enabled us to build up strong relationships with the kids. When we visited other youth centres, we realized that, although they outstripped what we could offer in the way of facilities, they couldn't beat us for warmth of fellowship and openness.

'The kids have shared their experiences. We've got into conversations about AIDS, sex and all the growing pains that they feel. For the first time in many years, the kids have been open to sharing themselves and their lives with other people.'

The club's refurbished premises were decorated by the young people themselves. They saw it as a responsibility, and carried it out with dedication and pride in their work. The results were so pleasing that they even invited their parents in to survey their handiwork!

Willy compares this with the redecoration of the Broadwater Farm Estate in Tottenham after the riots of 1985. This too was done by local youths who were so pleased their work that they physically discouraged any would-be graffiti artist from spoiling it! 'Perhaps the 'Y' Club's wall will similarly remain graffiti-proof!' Willy adds.

'The kids have done all the grafting. They've sensed that here is a centre for *them* to use. Their openness to talk, as they were working, was fantastic. A lot of the barriers have come down, basically through keeping at it on a one-to-one basis. Perseverance is the name of the game.'

As the young people went home fired with enthusiasm and a sense of achievement, their parents were also infected: a sense of 'something worthwhile' entered their lives. They were impressed to the point of rolling up their shirt sleeves and getting stuck in to the decorating themselves. Whole families were brought closer together through the sense of common purpose. Parents saw their children in a new light – as young adults capable of their own achievements, and of being emotionally committed to a project which commanded their time and loyalty.

Somewhere along the line, the gap between young people and their elders, which Willy expressed at the start of the refurbishment, was bridged. Even the children at the younger end of the club's range caught the vision. They picked up on the expectations of the older youngsters. There was a general sense of expectancy and enthusiasm.

'It's a privilege to be part of it all,' says Willy. 'I can't put it into words, but we've gone such a long way beyond my expectations of the way I'd hoped the work here would develop. The situation has changed so much even within the last twelve months. Even the management committee has changed as more local people have been able to get involved. The area is changing, churches are expanding – you have to get in early on Sundays, to get a seat – and it's like a revival happening.'

Willy makes a point of always arranging to meet any of the young people who want to go along to church. Sometimes he arranges a pick-up point and finds, on the day, that no one turns up. At other times, he finds a minibus load waiting. Many of the young people have become committed to the Christian way of life, and have made changes in their lifestyles.

'I get a lot of personal support, too, from the local churches, though I wish I knew precisely who is praying for my work and how often. A lot of my friends, particularly those who used to have some involvement here, pray for me regularly.

'It's a pity that some churches elsewhere still feel, "We've got a youth worker; let's let him get on with it." They don't see that the worker has needs, too. We can easily get left out on a limb and taken for granted.

'I need to be counselled occasionally. I can go to my vicar, and there are some other good local youth workers, but they're not all Christians.' One thing that Willy finds lacking is an opportunity for Christians in his type of work to draw together, to share needs and successes. However, he finds Frontier Youth Trust a great help, and Youth with A Mission have recently opened a centre nearby, to teach Christians and to serve as a training resource.

Willy looks back over his own successes with amazement: 'I'm now in a respected professional position, when once I was a leather-clad street kid. God has picked me up, and chosen me to do his work. I'm proud of the way the club development has progressed, and of the kids who have come to know Jesus, but I'm proudest of the simple fact that Willy Holland is doing this job, for God.

'The lad who was all for a bit of "aggro" and kickin' people's 'eads in is now looking to change people's lives. I'm ministering to kids who are the way I once was. I can tell them, "I've been there," and they'd suss me out if I was kidding them. They know I'm not.

'I'm just thankful for people like Pip Wilson, and other Christians who helped me. I just hope that I can do the same for others.'

5

Cannabis for breakfast

Martin Hardwidge – Andover

'Jasper was a drug addict who had been admitted to the drug unit at his local hospital literally hundreds of times for drug overdoses,' says Martin Hardwidge. 'He stayed at one of our re-habilitation units for a short time, then went off home again. A few days later, he overdosed once more and tried to get to the hospital – as usual. But on that last occassion, he didn't quite make it; he was found dead on a bench in the hospital grounds. It was so sad. He'd killed himself and he hadn't meant to do it; he had got to within twenty-five yards of help.

'Addicts do crazy things to conceal their activities. I know of a house full of young addicts who discovered that one of their number had died from an overdose on the premises, and desperately did not want the police involved. They carried the body a couple of streets away and propped it up on a doorstep in the middle of the night.

'That incident caused years of anguish for Anne, one of the addicts involved, who harboured the guilt feelings that were involved. Intensive counselling was needed by workers at another of our re-habilitation units before she could come to accept that she was not directly responsible for the death. When Anne eventually became a Christian, she was everyone's idea of an ideal convert; her hair colour changed from pink to brunette, her dress-sense became less outrageous, and her whole demeanour was transformed. Three years on, you really wouldn't believe that it was ths same person.'

Martin Hardwidge has, since 1977, been the General Secretary of the Coke Hole Trust – a Christian-run registered charity, based in Andover, in leafy Hampshire. The Coke Hole operates a hostel for home-less young people, a drop-in centre (originally for unemployed young people, but now with a wider brief), and three drug rehabilitation units – one for males, one for females, and one for mothers with chil-dren. Martin is self-depreciating about his job; despite the plush title, at times he feels more like the general dogsbody!

Barbara and Doug Henry were the original driving force behind the work. The Coke Hole began as a typical church youth club at the Andover Baptist Church during the 1960's. After a failed attempt to organize a meeting of all the youth clubs in Andover, to which no one turned up, Barbara and Doug – in true biblical fashion – went out and invited in some rowdy young people off the streets. From that none-too-prom-ising beginning grew a regular evangelistic coffee bar for the un-reached young people of Andover. It was held in the basement of the Baptist Church, in what had previously been the coke hole; hence the origin of the name.

The story has a second strand to it. While the Henrys were running the coffee bar, they were also serving as registered foster-parents. Some friends asked if they would consider taking Sandra, a London girl who needed a break in the country, to work for them as an au pair. The Henrys agreed, only to find that Sandra was a heroin adict.

Sandra found the Henrys to be so helpful and sympathetic that she asked Barbara to go to London to talk to some of her friends at a Soho nightclub. Barbara did so, leaving the nightclub at 3.00 am, deeply moved by a conviction that she should open her home to others like Sandra, who needed to move away from the closely knit London drug scene if they were to stand any chance of being rehabilitated.

By that time, the Henrys were already counselling, and sometimes offering temporary accommodation to, some of the young people who attended the Coke Hole coffee bar. There were drug-users there, too, and the Henrys quickly found themselves in need of a larger property. A benefactor stepped in to provide the money to purchase Ashley Copse, a large house in three acres of grounds in a rural area two miles from Andover. It was here that the work could continue.

In the early 1970's, Ashley Copse was run by a married couple and catered largely for young women ex-addicts. The Coke Hole Trust formally came into being to co-ordinate the work at Ashley Copse, and to begin a new work – a small hostel in New Street, Andover, for young people in need of accommodation where drug use was not involved.

The New Street building was only on a short-term lease, however, and in 1977 was demolished. The Trust to replace it, took over a building in Junction Road, Andover, which was made into a ten-bed hostel. This building, which had originally been a cottage hospital, had been used in turn as a police uniform store and a school dental clinic. It now operates as a hostel for single homeless young men in the 16–23 age range, as a piece of residential youth work.

A couple of years after Ashley Copse was founded, a second drug rehabilitation project was inaugurated. St. Vincent's, a slightly run-down house in six acres of grounds in a rural area a mile and a half from Andover, was purchased for the Trust by a second benefactor. St Vincent's houses up to nine men, compared with the eight women at Ashley Copse.

All the houses run on a family/community basis, with no internal hierarchical structure. Household chores and cooking are shared between staff and residents. During ths programme, staff live alongside residents, encouraging them to build up their own areas of interest. Throughout the programme, residents encounter situations that occur in everyday life. The Trust's approach is to rely on the staff setting examples for, and giving direction to, participants in the programme. A glimpse of St. Vincent's early work is provided by former addict Brian Greenaway, in his book *Hell's Angel:*

'Right from the start, they showed that they trusted me . . . I wasn't allowed to sit around doing nothing . . . After the morning chore, I'd be walking and talking and playing table-tennis with the other inmates (sic) at the hostel. They were mainly junkies who had kicked the habit and were trying to straighten themselves out. Other times I worked the overgrown garden ready for planting. I was also given charge of a pregnant goat that had been given to the project. All I got for my trouble were two baby he-goats!'

Livestock provide an integral part of the Trust's work. Apart from providing activity for the ex-addicts, caring for animals helps them to take responsibilities and to build relationships:

'Almost all the young people have had difficulty in establishing lasting relationships,' says Martin. 'They generally have a very low level of personal esteem. Part of the process of rebuilding self-confidence is to take care of something which makes demands – but not too many – on the person's time and commitment. An animal makes demands emotionally, but does not cause emotional hassle. It will acknowledge your existence and show that it likes you; that is very therapeutic. The way you may be feeling emotionally does not affect the animal's relationship with you; it may change its reactions, but the relationship itself will not be altered. You can't think that an animal has suspect motives, and is "out to get you" in the way you can about a human being. 'Looking after animals sets objectives that are not unreasonable, and which can be measured. Milking a goat is a recognizable goal. Meeting an objective is a way of restoring self-confidence.'

Aside from providing a stable environment for the rehabilitation of former drug-dependents, the 'rehab' houses run with two objectives: To provide the opportunities which will promote self-examination and individual assessment, and to assist individuals to realize their potential, recognize their worth, and arrive at an accurate opinion of their own ability to acheive selected goals in both the long and short term.

Staff seek to encourage responsibility in a number of areas, such as personal appearance, bedroom, chores and household maintenance. Many young people can, and do, experience a new dimension in their character development. They gain an awareness of what is happening in the group around them, and can glean some understanding what caring for others means, in contrast with their former drug-orientated condition, in which they are notoriously self-centred.

The programme evolves slowly to allow participants time to mature emotionally, to stablize and to develop both physical and mental faculties. Residents at the 'rehabs' can stay as long as necessary and this is usually at least a year to eighteen months. Throughout the programme, ex-addicts are assessed through regular staff meetings, and encouraged, challenged and supported by the staff who work with them. As time progresses, residents take on more reponsibility, both on a personal level in the resident group, and for the work allocated within the house. Opportunities for attending evening classes are available, and this has often been the preludes to enrolling for full-time educational courses.

There is a fundamental difference between the rehabilitation houses and the Junction Road hostel. Applying to a rehab is an acknowledgement that help is needed; therefore strict controls are imposed. At a hostel such as Junction Road, the only problem all residents admit to is the lack of anywhere to live. There are certain rules – young people eat together once a day, and must be in by a certain time at night – but within these, they remain firmly in control of their own lives. The hostel aims to move people on after approximately six months, though usually the residents need to find a job first; if they moved into a boarding house without being employed, they would be subject to the DHSS's unjust four-week rule, and constantly have to move on to other towns.

By the early 1980's, the Junction Road hostel was in full swing. Often friends would visit, and it was not uncommon for there to be thirty or more young people on the premises in any one evening. Part of the premises which were previously unused were converted for use as a drop-in centre. This was to cater for the needs of local young people, much as the original Coke Hole coffee bar (by that time, long since closed down) had done.

'Just at that point, the Manpower Services Commission announced their voluntary projects scheme,' Martin remembers. 'We got in on that and, for two years, under ever-changing ground rules, they paid us to run "BI Action" as a centre primarily for unemployed young people.'

Though Martin would never use the term when talking to the MSC, *B1 Action* was effectively a drop-in centre at that time – a place where a series of programmed activities took place with a regular, though ever-changing, group of young people. 'The scheme was not sufficiently rigorous for the MSC, so they pulled out after two years,' says Martin. 'At first, they gave us more staff than we asked for or needed. The second year, they gave us too few! At first, we could take the kids on leisure activities, then that was disallowed. Eventually, they pulled out at two weeks' notice, and since then *B1 Action* has been funded by voluntary donations.'

The difference between a drop-in centre and a youth club is an important one. Youth clubs *may* have an unemployment element attached to them, but drop-in centres like the Coke Hole's have the *specific intention* of working with unemployed young people. A youth club's aim is for education within leisure; whereas *B1 Action* provides education and support within *enforced* leisure.

'What began as a conventional drop-in centre has now developed a very specific client group which, though changing in people, is static in type. It is not about providing opportunities for the unemployed in the conventional MSC sense, but – on a very simple level – about being part of a family. It offers support and confidence rather than specific work-based opportunities. Its task is not so much to get people onto courses, as helping them to cope with life. It responds to the needs that are actually presented, rather than saying, "You are unemployed, that is your need, here is the solution." The level of counselling available to those who want it, is not dissimilar to that at the rehab houses,' says Martin.

'We try to help the young people to do whatever is their most pressing desire at the time. If they want to repair motor-cycles, we will help them to achieve that goal. If they have had a row with their girlfriend and want someone to talk with, we'll lend a listening ear. If you like, *B1 Action* is now a youth counselling service, that relates to up to 250 people per year – including probationary clients. But it runs photographic and screen-printing activities; there is a pool table and a coffee bar, too, so it has many of the aspects of a conventional drop-in centre. Its philosophy has to do with *being there* for people, and taking an interest in the whole person, rather than one small aspect of them, which might be that they are unemployed.'

B1 Action has had its fair share of troubles. In summer 1987, one of the young men with whom the project had been working died from inhaling vomit. He was a drug user in whom one of the Trust's workers had invested many hours of counselling and support, and his death came as a great shock to the *B1's* regulars. Many of them had not faced death so closely before and, already unsure, emotionally deprived, bewildered, hurt and unhappy, found the grief unbearable at first. They made a wreath themselves, and over fifty of them went to the funeral service, where the sermon was particularly appropriate.

Other incidents, though serious, have lighter over-tones. 'Some of the regulars burgled an electronics shop and stole some C.B. radios,' explains Martin. 'When they set off the burglar alarms in the process, they attempted to make their getaway on the nearest vehicle to hand – which happended to be a road digger! When they came back and told us that they'd been caught while trying to escape on a road digger, we couldn't believe that anyone would be *that* stupid!'

The most recent Coke Hole project to commence has been the mother-and-children unit, which has extended the Trust's ability to cope with female ex-addicts. The new unit, which was built on the land around Ashley Copse, was funded by the DHSS. This is the first of the Coke Hole's projects to have been built with statutory support; the other projects have always been initiated on a 'hand-to-mouth' basis.

'We don't hunt for referrals for any of the three rehabs, because we never have to. Clients are referred from every source imaginable: statutory bodies, health officers, probation officers, courts, families and ex-addicts themselves. A minority come from Christian sources. The accepted referral procedure is that an initial contact is made to ascertain whether we have, or are likely to have, a space. Then we ask the ex-addict to write to us. Only about one application in twenty would result in an interview; the application who seems to have some idea of their problem, and some motivation to be rehabilitated, is more likely to be invited for an interview.

'Typically, the interview would take half a day; it would be informal, but in depth. We would not take someone in on the day of the interview, but the acceptance rate after interview is high; we only interview if we have space. Usually, we would only turn someone down at that point if they had a long history of psychiatric disorder before the drug abuse started. Not all offers of places are taken up. Those we are not able to take in can apply elsewhere, but there are fewer beds available, overall, than there are young people in need of rehabilitation.'

Emotionally, many of the ex-addicts have not matured out of their teens, even though they may now be in their twenties or even thirties. Typically, they have been addicted for five years or more, and may have been addicted to any listed drug or, often, a combination. Most have had an opiate addiction, but many have tried anything and everything, from brass polish to heroin, to see what effect it has on them. They take drugs simply because they *like* what it does to them, though there is often a deeper reason, too:

'Some people take drugs because of the personality change that it induces. They perhaps feel more capable and have much more confidence in relationships if they are bolstered up with drugs. That is actually a very adolescent attitude – wanting to be someone that you are not. Others take drugs because it blots out unacceptable situations and enables them to cope with what would otherwise be intolerable emotional pressure. Sometimes, someone will start off as a pleasure-seeker and move to use drugs to become oblivious to the unpleasant things in life.'

It is true, though, that even non-users have similar desires and hang-ups, which are gratified by becoming reclusive, having sex, watching TV excessively, playing sport or going to concerts. Drug use can simply be an excessive – and socially unacceptable – means of achieving the stimulus or relaxation that the vast majority of people today are seeking, in order to be able to cope with everyday life. There are millions of people who use milder drugs such as valium, as a means of coping, and that extends into all walks of life.

Martin wonders whether there are some people who

use the church as a means of coping. 'A lot of people say, "Oh, I couldn't worship today, the service wasn't right." *Part of their faith is dependent on outside circumstances.* Just as a drug-user needs a particular drug in order to be able to cope with life, perhaps some Christians need a particular sort of church or type of worship.

'When someone says, "I didn't feel that God was in that sermon", I think, well, where *was* he then? Was it not really that the sermon didn't make them feel the way they felt the last time they thought they were really close to God? *Faith can be dependent on little things for reinforcement.* There's a parallel: Just as a Christian says, "I didn't feel as bored and browned off after the services at that other church," so the young addict says, "Oh, I felt much better able to cope when I was shooting up with heroin."

'Ex-addicts need to be shown what other options are open, and that other choices can be made. When people get into using drugs heavily, they limit their options for coping. Most of us develop a variety of means of dealing with an unpalatable situation, that reassure us that it is not the end of the world – but drug-users have been dependent solely on drugs. Ashley Copse is like St. Trinian's at times, and so it St. Vincent's. It's a sweeping generalization, but sometimes it is like living in a house full of adolescents; they just have not developed any alternative means of handling the stresses of everyday life.

'Some of the residents come from well-to-do families, who jet about all over the place. A lot of them come from very respectable, well-heeled backgrounds. Their drug use has not come from any need to blot out deprivation; in fact, a drug habit is so expensive to maintain that a wealthy background is probably the only alternative to crime as a means of supporting the habit. On many occasions, though, young people turn to drugs not *in spite of* their familes, but *because of* what has gone on in their family life.

'90% of the women who come through Ashley Copse have been incest victims, and that statistic is true of at least two other projects that I know. It is extraordinary! What do we have to offer a person like that? It's simply not enough to say, "Here's Jesus." That doesn't always take the pain and the hurt away. Often the ex-addicts feel they are a naughty little boy, or a dirty little girl, because it happened to them, and it was – they feel – their fault. But it is really *not* their sin; it has been visited upon them. They are carrying the guilt of it, and it needs to be brought out into the open. It's not nice to think that your own dad was a rat, but young people who have been incest victims need to learn that, in those circumstances, it's okay to have a pretty low opinion of your parents.'

There is not a programme, as such, for the rehabilitation process, though there is a pattern to it. The key to the way the Coke Hole operates is that it is very individual, because of the value that it attaches to the individual ex-addict. There are certain ground rules: 'A new resident is not allowed out of the grounds without a member of staff for the first three months. But we are not authoritarian; the staff don't wear white coats and go around with stethoscopes. We try to maintain a homely atmosphere.

'Everybody cooks, and everybody cleans – including the house staff, of which there are four in each house – there are no exceptions. Each house is responsible for purchasing food. Sometimes the meals will be concocted from a basic stock, and at other times menus will be planned, in detail, at the start of each week.

Surprisingly, perhaps, the standard of cooking in the girls' hostel is no different from that in the men's hostel, though the menus are noticeably different: in the women's house there tend to be more cakes around.'

It is not unknown for ex-addicts to try to smuggle drugs into the rehab house. At one staff meeting, Barbara Henry told how she had recently gone to wash her hands and found a plastic bag containing a large piece of cannabis sitting on the sink where its owner had absent-mindely left it. Barbara had promptly flushed it down the lavatory, much to the owner's consternation – it had cost him fifteen pounds! Other staff also had stories to tell about illegal substances being hidden in unlikely places: on one occasion, in a Corn Flakes packet!

'Drugs come in for a variety of reasons,' Martin expains. 'Friends in town think, "Poor old so-and-so, he's stuck out in the country. I'll send him a bit." We've had the stuff coming in inside cigarette packets and Mars bars. I'm not surprised by it. If someone's only coping mechanism is drug use, they are going to slip back occasionally. I think it would take someone with more strength of character than myself to come through without the occasional lapse.

'The first girl I remember who actually died through a lapse during rehabilition was doing very well until she went away to her parents for a weekend. On her way back, someone gave her a dirty fix. She thought that one little bit of dope wouldn't hurt, but she chose the wrong bit. She had everything going for her, but she blew it. Taking her last fix was literally the last thing that she ever did.'

Residents who repeatedly resort to drugs are warned about their conduct. If they show no real signs of giving up drugs, they are expected either to leave the project, or to agree to a more stringent regime designed to make it harder for them to slip back into their old lifestyle.

Another potential problem faced at the rehab houses is that of AIDS. Apart from sexual activity, the other common way in which the virus is transmitted is through infected hypodermic needles. Drug addicts, or former addicts are statistically more likely to be AIDS-postitive than other members of the population.

'I can't tell you whether we have any AIDS carriers in our hostels. There is no reason why we should know. We don't test people on admission, because it is pointless; the virus doesn't show up until three months after it has been caught – a carrier could have been on our premises, carrying the virus, for all that time.

'We treat *everybody* – including staff and visitors – as if they *were* AIDS carriers. It's the simplest option. We take all the precautions that we would take if we knew that someone was AIDS-positive. It's not arduous, no more than the precautions that we had been taking against hepatitis before AIDS came along.

The only real danger of spreading AIDS is through infected needles or sexual relations – neither of which the Trust encourages on our premises. Other than that, we just ensure that washing up is done properly, and that proper first-aid precautions are observed: disposable gloves have to be worn in certain circumstances, and old dressings must be burned. Those are sensible precautions which don't make the houses too institutionalized. We have never, yet, had a full-blown case of the actual illness.'

Physically, the young ex-addicts have been detoxified by a drug unit before arrival. They no longer have any physical dependency, though they can be – and often are – in poor physical condition. The first three months are spent trying to build up to a higher level of physical fitness, and to restore the sleep cycle – often the ex-addict's internal body clock is haywire. Little is expected of the resident during that time, though by the end, he or she would be expected to have developed relationships with other staff and residents – particularly with at least one staff member.

Counselling takes place informally. Sometimes outside specialist care is introduced say, for psycho-sexual counselling. There is no formal group work, though many aspects of such work are being worked on the whole time, through living in close proximity to other people in a tightly knit family situation. A need for more structured counselling has been recognized comparatively recently. The house staff no longer wear themselves out by dealing with each problem as it presents itself. They will, perhaps, say 'Let's talk about that at 3.00 pm tomorrow,' instead of breaking off from what they are doing immediately to lend a listening ear. 'The point of that,' says Martin, 'is that the residents learn that the sky won't fall on them if they have to wait a little while.' It teaches them to be patient and to recognize that other people have needs, too. In practice, residents have been known to unload the emotional baggage of lifetime on a staff member in the middle of the night – though this is actively discouraged!

The Trust employs two full-time social workers, who work across all the projects. They are both female, as are some of the live-in staff. They feel that some of the male residents at St. Vincent's are sexist in their attitudes. 'It is a sweeping generalization, but many of the guys who come to stay at St. Vincent's have not exhibited tremendously successful relationships with the opposite sex,' says Martin. 'They do not expect women to be strong, or to oppose them by saying, "I'm sorry, but you cannot do that now." Their

unspoken rule, that a man is in charge of his relationships, is challenged.

'That rule is not a helpful one, but they feel threatened
when it is challenged. It is, obviously, more acceptable
for a resident to get mad and, say, smash a window in
response to the felt threat, than to attack someone else
in the house. But the instances of that type of thing
becoming a reality are very rare: abuse is more likely
to be verbal. Verbal aggression is bad enough; one of
the female workers has commented that she can handle
it from women, but from men even verbal aggression
can feel physically threatening.'

The four workers who live at each house receive free
board and lodging, plus a salary linked ot the nationally
agreed levels for social workers, but they are available
on a round-the-clock basis. Much of the time, little
more is demanded of them than would be required in
any ordinary family home. So, seen in terms of living
in a family in which they have a specialist role, it is a
good deal. In terms of a job, working approximately
fourteen hours per day, for six days of the week (with
one weekend off per month, and five weeks leave per
year) it is a very bad deal. The worker's attitude is
important, as the conflict between being a family
member and a professional worker is not easily
resolved. A sense of community helps to make the
unacceptable bearable, though the job is still tiring and
taxing. 'Getting heavy theologically, it's about
kingdom values, not worldly values,' says Martin.

The Trust does not seek particular academic qualifications from its workers, though they should ideally
have experince of working with people. Some have
been nurses, others detached youth workers or teachers;
Lorna, one of the senior social workers, was formally
an RAF chaplain's assistant. The right attitude, and a

capacity of empathize (not sympathize) with the ex-addict are the crucial qualities that a worker must possess. They must be in touch with their own feelings and humanity.

House staff normally work for the Trust for at least two years – stability is important for the residents, and a rapid turnover of staff would be counter-productive. 'Most people experience problems in working for the Trust,' says Martin, 'but if you can see the job as an exercise in growth, you can come through the problems. Though the job challenges normal values, it offers real scope for personal growth. It affirms people.

Speaking for himself, Martin says that working for the Coke Hole Trust has significantly affected his own outlook on life: 'There were a lot of things attached to my faith that were really little bits of excess luggage. It was well worth being rid of them! Leaving it all behind when other people were still carrying a few suitcases was not pleasant; it made me feel that my relationship with God was cracking up – how could I still be a Christian if I no longer believed in those little "extras"? The extras tended to be the silly little cultural ways of expressing faith which make up much of the structure of Western church life, when all that is needed is simple biblical faith.'

One part of the baggage consists of having to believe that you will always get something out of a church service. Martin remembers growing up in the Brethren, and feeling an enormous sense of unburdening when someone else expressed the view – which he had been keeping inside – that the services were really boring! 'It was such relief for me to hear it said out loud.' There is a piece of baggage in Christian counselling, for example, that requires the counsellor to say, 'Shall we pray about your problem?' 'There is nothing wrong with that', comment Martin, 'except where the counsellor really means, "I haven't got a clue what to do about this problem," and is not prepared to admit it.'

Martin has found himself to be a lot more honest about his faith these days: 'There is no strong pressure on the ex-addicts to become Christians, apart from the fact they live in a house with four of them. It would be lovely to believe that all they have to do is to accept Christ and their troubles will be over; but the idea that it is really that simple is another piece of luggage that can usefully be lost.

'There is no set pattern but, for some ex-addicts, finding a relationship with God can be the factor that unleashes the capacity for other relationships. With others, they need first to accept that it is possible to *have* stable relationships, in order to be able even to understand God's desire to have a relationship with them.

'For one guy in the hostel at the moment – let's call him Stuart – it is a revelation to him that God is prepared to take him exactly as he is and that, if he blows it, God will *still* be prepared to take him as he is. That knowledge has opened up his ability to relate to other people. He still has the most disgusting vocabulary of obscene words that I've ever heard in my life, and using them is one way in which he sometimes blows it. He is now learning to handle that problem, though I would not yet be prepared to have him tell his testimony – which would make a good six pages in *The Sun* newspaper – in the way he usually relates it, to an average chuch congregation. Whatever the Holy Spirit may have done in his life, it has not yet filtered through to his vocabulary!'

Many of the Coke Hole staff are cynical about the way Christian books and articles tend to present the testimonies of ex-addicts who become Christians. Very often, they set up young convert up as some kind of super-Christian and put him on a pedestal. When he falls off, people don't know what to do with him. 'It is silly to think that, because he has been saved from worse sins than most people have dreamed of, he is somehow a "better" Christian.'

Another convert, Margaret, went on to run a drug-rehabilitation project of her own, in Scotland: 'She got her act together very quickly in terms of being able to really understand and relate to other Christians. Because she had a very good understanding of herself, she could see through other people when the need arose. Within twenty-four hours of her conversion, Margaret was different person. She just marched through her rehabilitation, and was fine.'

Some of the residents show no signs of responding to the Christian faith during their period of rehabilitation, and many, when they leave, do not want to have anything further to do with Coke Hole. Others have fond memories, and occasionally revisit. One staff member has specific responsiblity for follow-up of ex-residents who want to keep in touch. The numbers involved are very small, with perhaps only five or six people leaving each house in a given year.

One of the biggest difficulties encountered by residents who become Christians during their stay is coping with the church. Not only Coke Hole, but many other projects, cite this as a difficulty, and Martin has some clear ideas why this should be so. 'Many denominational bodies are frightened by frontier youth work,' he believes. 'Ministers feel threatened by workers who operate outside their church situtations, because they are not subject to their rule. That's my opinion.

'Most of the social action by Christians in the last

couple of centuries has started *outside* the established denominations. It's strange, but workers from the Trust, visiting other churches, find themselves almost in the position of overseas missionaries on furlough. People think that, because you work for a professional Christian organization, you must be some sort of spiritual superstar! It's absolute drivel, but people still come up and say piously, "I think your work is wonderful." Perhaps that's so that they don't have to do anything about it themselves!'

Many of the Trust's staff are critical of evangelical cliques, and of individual Christians who live out their Christian life through reading or hearing about other people's work, instead of doing something themselves.

Frontier youth work requires a depth of commitment that is costly, and sometimes uncomfortable even to read about. Taking care of young people's physical needs as a way of sharing Christ's love requires patience, and time set aside without distraction, but it is well worth the effort!

6

Bibles in their back pockets

George Watson – Edinburgh

Pilton sprawls to the north of Edinburgh, a couple of
miles out from the town centre. Its dominant colours
are off-white and grey; though there is more grass than
one would find, say, in an urban priority area near to
the heart of a city. One particularly ugly council estate,
grey with a few red panels, resembles a concentration
camp.

Weeds grow between the paving stones, the roads
show signs of having been dug up repeatedly, and the
walls are covered in graffiti. Other eyesores include
privet hedges untrimmed for years, empty houses,
mutilated road signs, rubbish skips, overgrown
gardens, overflowing drains, bare breeze blocks, and
rusting scaffolding. Pop music blares from windows. It
is not the sort of place where most people would want
to bring up children.

St David's is a very ordinary whitewashed church
building situated at the end of a long straight road. In
the other direction are three more churches squatting
next to the road, the nearest only about forty yards
away. Inside St David's, George Watson is waiting.

'Seventy per cent of the housing in the area has been
built by the council, and sold off to owner-occupiers,'
George explains. '1,500 people in the area are addicted

to mainline drugs. This has led to a serious AIDS problem, the disease being contracted through addicts sharing unsterilized needles rather than through sexual misdemeanours.

'From the last figures I was able to get, 100 people in Edinburgh were expected to die of AIDS during 1987. Of the women tested who would be classed as prostitutes, the latest figures show 500 to be AIDS-positive. Many of them are drug addicts themselves, who sell their bodies to pay for their daily fixes.'

George first worked in the Pilton area during the late 1970's, handling a heavy social work case-load. His tasks were made no easier by the local authority's decision to put all its problem families into the area. That led to continual deterioration of facilities. Those who could afford to move away did so, leaving behind all the poorest and most socially deprived families.

When he was working for the local authority, George was obliged to work their way. However much he may have wanted to share Christ with these people, he had to keep within statutory guidelines; the authority would not take kindly to him going about peddling Christianity. 'There are a lot of Christian social workers in the area, and they find continued conflict over how far they can share their faith.'

One girl on George's case-load was twenty-seven years old, with three children by different fathers. The children grew up not knowing who their father was; any male who went into the home ended up being called 'Daddy'. Clearly, any support and guidance that she might have expected from a youth worker during her developing years had not been present. It was her children who needed a youth worker's support now. The girl worked as a strip-tease dancer, and kept pythons, a monkey and a puma in her flat!

'I still remember on my first visit, seeing the puma in the corner of the living room. That was enough for me! I was off! The trouble was that she had no respect for herself – she didn't see any value in herself. Sharing Jesus with her would have been one answer, but you couldn't do that as a local authority worker. I was there simply to do an enquiry into why the children kept missing school.

'To work successfully with a girl like that, you need to devote a great deal of time. If you're carrying sixty or sixty-five families on your case-load, you just cannot invest the necessary time. I felt that the local churches could have done something. The social services actually approached one church and asked for the use of their church hall one evening per week and on Saturdays, to run clubs staffed by the authority's social workers. The reply from the local minister was: 'We've just had our floor polished, and we don't want those kids messing it up!'

'In the end, we rented a disused shop in which to run the clubs. The sad thing was the way the churches were so ineffectual. In fairness, the Roman Catholics did a lot of work, and one of the Church of Scotland churches was fairly active. But for the rest,' George shakes his head, 'their approach was abysmal. That's created a lot of problems, because you've got these lovely buildings not being fully utilized, in an area where there are very few facilities. I think the church here has a lot to answer for!

'Secondly, at that time the congregations lived outside the area, drove in to worship, then returned to the suburbs. They couldn't see the church in its true role – of being *in* the community, to *serve* the community.'

Eight years ago, the concept of Kingdom Theology was non-existent among the churches here, though by the end of the 1980's, the situation had changed. Churches were becoming supportive – they were beginning to identify with the needs of the community, and to speak out against social injustice.

While George was working in Pilton as a social worker, however, he found the situation so negative that he left and went to Aberdeen to be ordained as a minister.

'I felt that the Lord was calling me into the ministry in the Church of Scotland. During the training, I left the Church of Scotland and joined the Baptists – because of doctrine. Though I had no basic intention of coming back to Edinburgh – I would like to have looked at churches in the north-east, and I certainly wasn't looking to move back into a youth ministry – the Lord changes things!

'In 1980 I saw an advertisement for a worker to provide Christian input – Bible studies and worship services – for young people in the East End of Edinburgh. My interest in the job stemmed from my social work background. I wanted to try to relate Christianity directly to youth work.'

George applied for the post and was interviewed. He was not sure that it was the right move for him, but he was offered the job anyway. He prayed about it, and it seemed the right thing to do.

The project was sponsored by the Edinburgh Council of Churches, and based at Hillside church, which was then in a run-down working class area, with many of the problems that George had experienced only a mile or two away in Pilton. As the name suggests, the church was set on the side of a hill, which dominated Edinburgh's East End. The Playhouse Theatre stands at one side, and dilapidated Georgian houses jostled around it. George gave an initial commitment to work with the project for two years; but, every time he has thought about leaving, the appropriate doors into other areas of ministry have not opened.

'Basically, we ran a youth cafe. We worked with board games, arts, drama and silk-screen printing, as well as the Christian activities. Our brief was to work with the homeless and unemployed. There were many bed-and-breakfast houses in the area, where those sort of people congregated. It was a policy decision to work with 16–24 year olds, since that is an age range for which there is otherwise a notable lack of facilities in Edinburgh.'

The project worked with thirty to forty people at any one time, in eighteen different groups each week – all of which were well attended. Typically, a session might involve role plays on how to behave at job interviews; how to complete DHSS forms; and discussions about Third World and political issues.

The weekly Bible study began with twelve young people the first week. Seven came back the second week, and four the third. George and two voluntary workers prayed about the situation, and concluded that they ought to run the studies along the lines of a discussion group. It worked. Attendance gradually increased until thirty unchurched young people were studying the Bible each week. By the end of the project's second year, George was having to run Bible studies four times a week to keep up with the demand.

'We had some kids who were making a round trip of sixty miles to come to a Bible study. It was gratifying, but we were sad that they were not able to get that kind of Bible study locally. *They* set the topics, and the studies were like debates. We discovered that, in order for them to argue against our case, they had to go away and read the scriptures – and that was the way to get the Bible across to them.'

The project was quite successful in the number of people who became Christians. Some of them joined local Edinburgh churches, while those from further afield moved to churches in their own community. Those who fell away tended to be those who went to city-centre evangelical churches where skinhead haircuts and leather jackets were conspicuous among the suits.

Duncan Cox was one male with whom the project worked. He was very fond of his mother, but antagonistic towards his father – to an extent that was putting stress on their marriage. When Duncan's father wanted to throw him out of the house, his mother came to his support, and threatened to leave too. It was only at the age of twenty-one, when his parents had another child, that the situation began to improve: suddenly he was no longer the centre of attention. He had never been deceitful – just economical with the truth, and with well developed powers of manipulation.

Then he was injured in a road accident. Duncan maintained that God spoke to him while he was in hospital, and he became a baptized member of a city-centre church. Sadly, Duncan fell away again, possibly because the church was unable to cope with him. Duncan had changed. He had bought a suit and adapted to a middle-class lifestyle to fit in with what he saw in the church around him. Perhaps it was the artificiality of that which finally drove him away. The 'Christian clone' syndrome happens in Edinburgh as elsewhere. The story reminds us of Noel Hunter's account of Patrick in Belfast.

Other young people are converted too easily. They accept Christ, but do not understand the effect that they must allow that to have upon their lifestyles. George knows of girls who have resumed sleeping with their boyfriends within days of being baptized. Many are emotionally disturbed; they come from broken homes, and lack love. They see Jesus *as* love – but a wishy-washy, sentimental love, far removed from the sacrificial love of a dying saviour.

At one point, a Teddy-boy gang operated around the city centre. It took the view that any girls in the gang belonged to the gang, and that any male had the right to sleep with any girl. She had no choice in the matter if she wished to remain in the gang. When George and his co-workers made it clear that this was not right, they met with various degrees of verbal abuse. One girl, called Karen, went to him one day screaming: 'You've explained Christianity to my boyfriend, 'and now he says that he won't sleep with me until we get married!'

Of all the teenage subcultures George has worked with, he believes that skinheads respect girls most. They give women a dignity quite unlike, say, Teddy-boys or bikers, who treat the opposite sex like part of the furniture until it is time for a gang-bang. Skinheads tend to be more articulate and less aggressive, George has found, than other youth cultures.

'We worked with a girl who was badly disfigured. Claire was her name. She was horrific to look at, and mentally retarded in some respects – though she knew how to look after money! She was frequently abused, sexually, by young men who exploited her low self-esteem. Typically, they would feign affection in order to get her into bed.'

Claire became pregnant by one of these men. When she gave birth, the child was taken into care for its own safety – she was thought to be unable to look after it. George argued strongly that she should be given the opportunity to *prove* herself a fit mother, and the courts gave her the baby under a very strict supervision order; but, within six weeks, it became clear that she could not manage.

Caroline came to the project frightened and confused because her boyfriend was a drug addict. She did not want to give up her sexual relationship, but was worried about contracting AIDS. George had to work through all the moral, psychological and social implications with her. She was aware of spiritual implications, too: Caroline was a searcher after Christ, although she had always drawn back from making any firm Christian commitment. All George and his team could do was to counsel her about her AIDS worry, pray for her, and be around when she needed someone to whom she could freely talk.

'Others have come right through, sorted out their lives and joined the church,' George is pleased to say. 'They can become a big support in this kind of ministry. When they've been on drugs, into the gang scene and everything else, they can break down barriers for us much more quickly than we are able to do. They are 'known'.

'We've had times when the local police have come in and asked, "What have you done with these kids? We've told them to move on and they've moved. We're no longer getting any verbal abuse!" At other times, the local press have asked how we were able to have skinheads, mods, head-bangers, and all the other groups, at the centre without fighting breaking out. Word had trickled out that it was a place where you could go, and be accepted for what you were. The local authority used to get concerned when the kids started wandering about with Good News Bibles in their back pockets!'

One of the few rules which the project imposed was that no one under the influence of alcohol – however little – was allowed on the premises. That was made clear from the beginning and, in the seven years that the project has been running, only about ten people have been turned away.

'We've had people with drug problems. They've needed a lot of support, and somewhere to come when the pressure has been on them. We've seen people come off drugs, but it's difficult to give them the long-term support that they need.'

Among the most serious issues which George and his team have come up against have been homelessness and housing problems. Young people have been threatened by their landlords with assault, if they went to an agency to report the conditions in which they were living. On occasions, physical violence has actually resulted. One person was paying £35 per week in rent, to live in an out-house, which was a converted coal cellar. Another was paying the same to live in a tent in the back garden.

The old trick of paying landladies for the use of a postal address is common. Landladies have charged twenty pounds for an address to which giros could be sent and collected. When George contacted the local DHSS office, he was told that nothing could be done about the unscrupulous landladies, though the young people could be charged with fraud.

In 1984, the project had its own homelessness problem. The Church of Scotland sold off the Hillside church and the project was forced to move to less suitable premises in the High Street – on the Royal Mile from Edinburgh Castle to Holyrood House.

Fire regulations meant that they had to work with fewer people in the building. Because the project was one of the few agencies that worked at night, it began to attract alcoholics off the street, who were over its age limit; that, in turn, began to deter the young people from coming.

'We had to start moving the alcoholics on,' says George, 'to get the young folk back. The property belonged to the local authority, and was far from ideal. Entry was via an entryphone system. Thirty of the forty people we'd worked with at Hillside had found employment – by walking around every factory in Edinburgh, knocking on doors and asking for a job. At the High Street, we had basically a completely new set of people with whom to work.'

Four years into the project, George had two full-time workers alongside him – until one was tragically killed in a car crash, and the post was frozen. The project went through a financial crisis for the next three years.

When the local authority put the High Street property on the market, after two years, the project was homeless again. Roger Simpson, the Rector of 'P and G's' – St Philip's and St George's church – offered them the use of their church hall located, ironically, only a stone's throw from the project's original Hillside base.

Upon moving in, the project inherited a group of young people who had been attracted to P and G's youth cafe. These young people lived mainly with their parents, and wanted nothing more than a glorified youth club – but the project was much more than that. In the one year the project spent based at P and G's, it experienced more break-ins and vandalism than in the previous six.

'The young people constantly wanted to get their own way. Then, when the government enforced its ruling requiring unemployed young people to move on after four weeks in bed-and-breakfast establishments, if they wished to continue claiming benefit, those establishments decided to take in only people aged over twenty-six. The project's basic core group was being driven out of the East End.

A couple of shopping centres where young people used to congregate were now closed in the evenings. With nowhere to go, still more of the young people, even those with jobs, began to move away.' George began to wonder if there was any future for the project. Perhaps it had run its course and was ready to be terminated.

There were other problems, too. All the churches in Edinburgh supported the project financially, but the money they gave in a year would not support the project for two weeks; most of the finance came from outside agencies and trusts. The number of times that the local clergy visited the project in a year could be counted on the fingers of one hand. Roger Simpson – who had been on the staff at All Souls, Langham Place, and was familiar with the work of the All Souls Club House – was more committed. He could obviously see the value of the project's work and, having recently arrived, he was less set in his ways. Only while the project was based at P and G's did it receive, at last, a substantial contribution from local Christians towards its running costs, because P and G's paid the project's lighting and heating bills.

P and G's was coming to life. The congregation had grown from a few dozen to a few hundred. Already the project was restricted in the number of weekday evenings that it could operate, due to the church's own demands on its premises. It was clear that the demand was going to grow still further as the church continued to expand. If the project was to re-establish itself with its original aims intact, it would need its own premises again. The work is such that access needs to be available virtually around the clock.

Additionally, as the East End was becoming more and more gentrified – through the dilapidated Georgian houses being renovated and converted into modern flats – working-class young people began to move out of the area, to be replaced by the Scottish equivalent of the Sloane Ranger set. The older tenements were all demolished, and it looked as though it was right for the project to close completely, leaving P and G's to run their own community-based programme from their own hall.

At a meeting on a Tuesday evening, the project's Chairman suggested that, before closing down operations for good, enquiries should be made to see if there was any other area to which they could move. The next morning, a minister in the West Pilton area approached George and asked if he would consider returning to Pilton to run a youth ministry there. 'I said that I would think about it, and that was all. I tried to forget about it! But, more and more, the idea kept coming back, so I said, "Okay, let's do a background report." We visited local groups, clergy and statutory agencies. We walked and walked the area till we had the feel of it. I had the advantage of having worked here, and some of the local hard men still remembered me! We researched the crime rates and the drug rates to justify coming here. The more work that we did, the more people said, "Yes, we want you to come," and that was even the non-Christian agencies.'

Within ten days of deciding to move to Pilton, and to recommence the project from there, the project's bank account rose from £7 to over £26,000! People were not simply *saying*, 'Come', they were backing up their requests with their money, to show they meant business this time.

There have been many changes since George worked there in the 1970's. Part of West Pilton has become gentrified, but most of it is still very run down. Drug abuse and prostitution are still rampant – one woman runs a brothel only a couple of streets from the project's new base. Yet the churches are finally beginning to work together. The local Bapstist church is particularly supportive, and so too is St. David's, which has provided the project with premises in its hall, and the local Catholic and Church of Scotland churches.

The project plans a significant input into local mums-and-toddlers groups, because of the high proportion of single-parent families in the area, to which the project wishes to relate. A new worker has been recruited and, at the end of 1987, the project is under way again in its new home, with an agenda that includes welfare rights, Bible studies, housing benefits, aerobics, arts and crafts, mums-and-toddlers and various discussion groups. The input on AIDS and drug abuse is being kept at a low level to avoid scaring people away. More volunteers are needed to help with the project: 'One of the problems with youth ministry,' says George, 'is that ordinary people don't realize that *anyone* can contribute. They don't have to be professionals.'

For George Watson, the events of the last ten years have come full circle. Geographically, he is back where he started; but a lot of progress has been made along the way. Like Noel, John, Martin, Maureen and Willy, he has found that frontier youth work is not a tough option. Tough, it undoubtedly is; but, for a committed Christian surrounded by needy young people, it is *not* optional.

7

It's the bloody führer!

Rosie Towers – Harrogate

Belfast, London, Liverpool, St Helens and Edinburgh are the sort of situations we associate with frontier youth work; Andover, in leafy Hampshire, perhaps less so. But middle-class Harrogate, home of affluent businessmen who commute into work in the Yorkshire cotton towns, must be about the last place one would expect to encounter such work!

Neither is Rosie Towers the sort of person that one immediately thinks of as a youth worker. A grandmother, though still in her thirties, and prone to explosive bursts of laughter, Rosie lives with her extended family, which includes four mentally handicapped foster-adults. 'The household never goes above ten,' she explains, 'You would lose the point then, because it becomes too big for a family, and you don't have the time to spend with people.' Her aim is to give to those who do not have a family – and perhaps never have had – a warm, caring, family environment.

'Two of the foster-adults are forty-three, one is thirty-five and the other – who is also physically handicapped – is thirty-nine. Then we usually have one or two lads with us, who have been into drugs or some other bother. I also have two children of my own – and a wonderfully patient, amazing husband!

'Generally speaking, Harrogate is a bit posh. This street is particularly straight-laced – all pin-stripes and bowler hats. When we moved in, we had two boys staying with us who had massive great mohican hair-cuts, and a punky daughter who, half the time, had almost no hair. The neighbours got a bit of a fright!'

Rosie was a Samaritan before she became a Christian. Her life was transformed upon her conversion, in the late 1970's. Shortly after, she felt that God seemed to be calling her to stop being a Samaritan: 'I said "No!", Rosie laughs, warmly, 'God said, "Well, you really should. It's time you left," and I said, "Well, I'm not going till you tell me what you want me to do." It went on like that for about six months until I was absolutely worn out, and not particularly happy.'

Eventually, she decided to give in and let God be Lord in her life. After a restful few months, she heard that a YMCA was about to start in Harrogate. It immediately made her think of the dirty old YMCA building in her native Manchester. At the time she wondered why the 'C' stood for 'Christian', since it didn't seem to her to be a particularly Christian organization.

Then a friend telephoned her to say that the YMCA would be starting an Intermediate Treatment Group for young people. Was Rose interested in becoming involved as a helper? 'I felt that it was what God wanted me to do. It was only for a set length of time – nine months, I think. In the middle of that time was an open meeting for local churches, when interested people came together for discussion. We split up into groups to discuss the topic "What do you want the YMCA to mean to you?" We actually ended up with a list of the YMCA's original aims and purposes written down, though none of us had seen the original document.

Harrogate YMCA was an experimental project to get back to the organization's original aims and purposes. It was intended to be a group of Christians wanting to share the gospel by doing something useful in the community; people committed to the *ideal* rather than just to the specific task.'

At about the same time, Rosie had discussed with a group of friends the possibility of running a youth coffee bar in the town. They prayed about it and, eventually, when the Harrogate YMCA was fully operational, Rosie and some friends – who had been running a mixed physically handicapped/physically able social club on a large estate – felt that the time seemed right:

'About six of us prayed together and decided that, if it *was* right, there were certain resources we would need. They were: volunteers, finance and expertise – none of which we had! It was like "putting a fleece before the Lord",' she says, echoing Gideon in Judges 6:36–40. 'We thought, "If it's right, God will provide." '

Two days later, Rosie received a mysterious phone call. To this day, that person remains anonymous, but an offer was made to provide some money, '. . . in case you, er, get a building together, or something.' Another member of Rosie's prayer group received a call from someone offering their services as a volunteer helper.

' "I've had enough of this praying business," I thought. "Too much happens!" A few days later, my husband and I were chatting with a group of people in our lounge. I didn't know them very well, but one of them turned around and said to me, "Do you know that project you're involved in? You ought to have a building. If you ever get one, I'm the manager of a housing association, and I'll give you a hand with the lease." ' Volunteers, finance and expertise had all come forward. Not yet enough to run the project, but God had clearly answered their prayers.

Rosie and her colleagues eventually secured the lease on a terraced house in a row called Cheltenham Parade, which was being gradually converted into a row of shops. It needed to be accessible by wheelchair – not because the project was specifically geared for physically handicapped people, but because they felt that it was wrong to exclude them. The catchment consisted simply of those young people whom no one else wanted; who had either been excluded from the youth club scene, or who did not wish to be a part of it.

It was a drop-in centre, open for a part of most days, run entirely by voluntary staff – except for the final two years of the project, when two workers were employed under the auspicies of the Manpower Services Commission.

Funding was 'prayed in': 'We needed an electric fire, so I went out and bought one. At midnight that night, a gentleman I'd met *once* phoned up a mutual friend, who answered the phone, bleary-eyed. A voice on the other end asked if I was praying for anything in particular. "I don't know what she's praying for! Send her some money!" He sent us £100, and the electic fire had been £99.

'It was like that all the time. When we were setting up the building, we prayed, made a list of all the items that we would need and advertised for them in the local newspaper; only we inadvertently left off the list some brown carpet that we needed. Someone phoned up apologizing that she didn't have *any* of the items for which we'd advertised. "But," she said, "I do have a bit of brown carpet"!'

The project continued to be run on prayer, as planning progressed towards the opening of the drop-in centre and coffee-bar. Not all the helpers had to be Christians, though Rosie was very careful to maintain a balance. Anyone who was actually opposed to the kingdom was discouraged from being involved.

James, a volunteer about whom Rosie had reservations, drove a minibus full of young people at eighty miles per hour on a motorway, wrecked the minibus – fortunately, without anyone being injured – and abandoned it, and the young people, in the pretext of going off to look for help. After discussing the matter with local FYT worker Greg Thompson, Rosie decided that James had to go. 'Many Christians are too wishy-washy. Loving people is not a wishy-washy business. If you are doing what God wants, then you get attacks from the enemy. You've got to expect it, and to pray against it.

'You have to work the right way around, and seek what God is wanting. Then you have to pray and say, "We'd really like you do to this, Father," because God is a gentleman, and he likes to be asked. I know he knows; but it's like my kids, I love them to say "I love you". I know that they love me, and I love them, but we tell each other *every* day.'

Another of Rosie's helpers, Philip, was a teacher of classics at Wakefield Grammar School. He travelled to Harrogate every Friday evening, stayed the night as part of Rosie's extended family, and was the Saturday leader at the drop-in centre. Though not a Christian, he was very much in favour of the project. He is now working with boys in refugee camps in Oman for the Quaker movement, in close contact with the YMCA. He has discovered that there is something more to life than collecting endless academic qualifications.

Bill, a gentle Scot approaching retirement, was also a non-Christian who worked as a volunteer on the project. 'You've even got *me* thinking that there's something in this Christianity lark,' he said, before leaving to work in Scotland. He later retired back to Harrogate to nurse his dying wife. Shortly after his wife died, Rosie found herself desperately short of volunteer helpers and, in trepidation, rang Bill. 'How do you do it?' asked Bill on the telephone. 'I was standing here, thinking, "the wife's dead, all the affairs are in order, what am I going to do now?" ' Working at the drop-in centre again gave his life much-needed direction and, through the centre, he eventually became a Christian.

When a petite and apparently frail old lady offered to help, Rosie thought, 'The lads will eat her!' But she proved to be a very effective volunteer, whom the young people came to look upon as a surrogate grandmother. They would open doors and carry cups for her. 'She was a great old character,' Rosie remembers, 'slightly deaf, which wasn't a bad thing when the lads started using ripe language. She'd smile and ask "What did you say?" and the lads would go, "Oh, it's a nice day." '

Rosie herself has a novel way of dealing with bad language. When young people say, 'Oh God! or 'Oh Christ!' in her presence, she retorts, 'He must be getting sick of hearing you say that by now. You say "Oh God", and he says "Yes", then you say nothing else. He never gets a sentence out of you!' Like many other workers, Rosie has found that good humour can always defuse a tense situation. 'Sometimes, confronted by a large group of aggressive lads, I've been momentarily unnerved. But I've just had to remember that God is bigger than them all.'

The centre comprised a coffee-bar on the ground floor, and various rooms on the two floors above, though the top floor was used so infrequently that it was eventually let out as a self-contained flat. There were times, particularly on Saturdays, when the drop-in centre was packed, often with a mixture of skinheads, greasers and gangs from other teenage subcultures. But some of the quieter times were the best, when there was more time to spend talking with people individually.

'Another of the difficulties, as Pete Stow points out in the book *Youth in the City*, is that one gang occasionally dominates, and the place becomes theirs. We didn't really want that.' There was often quite enough trouble stemming from the activities of certain of the members:

'There was a safe in the cellar. It had only about fifteen quid in it, but some lads pinched it – not the money, the whole safe! They hired a get-away car, which must have cost them more than the safe's contents. Then they spent hours trying to crack it open; they didn't know that it was all rusty and could be opened just by knocking the top!'

Simon was the leader of the would-be safe-crackers. Five feet ten inches tall, with holes in his jeans, no hair, few front teeth and lots of tattoos – he was a tough nut, but Rosie knew how to frighten him. 'I just had to say, "If you don't stop that, I'll give you a cuddle!" He would squirm with embarrassment, and I would say, "I'll just *have* to hug you!" '

Rosie and her team would never condone their aggressive, and often criminal, activities – but they kept on loving them just the same. Money was stolen and fire extinguishers misused, but nothing was allowed to destroy the friendships that were forged. 'I'd love to say that they all became Chrsitians and lived happily ever after, but it wouldn't be true. Some were converted and some weren't, but we've no doubt that God gave them a different life – though some of them have still to do a lot of changing.'

100

Jim was one of the few youths who could make Rosie feel uncomfortable; he had a bad reputation for being very unpleasant. 'We prayed about him to the point where I though "Oooh! I'm going to have to hug you *too*, Jim" He became a Christian and settled down in a local church. Everything was okay for a while, and he behaved himself. But he ended up in trouble again. He got married, divorced, went to prison . . . Golly! But he's still "different". God is still working there somehow. He's now out on remand. Maybe he needed to be in prison to separate him from the gang with which he was associated. I hear that he has been spreading the gospel in jail!'

Rosie worked with a family of four children, all with the same mother, but different fathers. There was a different man in the house every few weeks. The children were beaten by one of the men for allegedly stealing some money though they had seen *him* take it. The mother was a very likeable person – when she was sober. With such a family upbringing, it was inevitable that they would grow up maladjusted. The oldest, Ian, has a serious drink problem, and all the brothers have been fostered by Rosie, and her husband Nigel, at one time or another.

Ian was the first to be fostered. He had been in a detention centre, and came out to find himself homeless; his family had been split up, with his mother in a psychiatric hospital and his younger siblings taken into care. He went to stay with Rosie's extended family for three weeks, and left after two and a half years!

'There is very little by way of accommodation for single people in Harrogate,' says Rosie. 'For single girls with children, it is a little better; for single men, there is nothing – I know of one guy who sleeps under a college stage. It is good that people can buy their own council houses, but it does reduce the housing stock and there are not enough council houses already.

'People will say that alcohol, unemployment and drugs are the worst problems for young people in Harrogate. But the real problem is the absence of Jesus in their lives. It is that which shows up in the excessive use of alcohol, glue, drugs and the like. Much of the trouble that young people get into happens when they are intoxicated. Two lads beat up a plain clothes policeman, another attacked his own wife; many steal for excitement, or to feed their particular habit.

'Charges of actual bodily harm and grievous bodily harm are all too disastrously common. I've had lads brought to me who are plain ill from drinking the wrong things – like cider, topped up with pond water – or from drug abuse. Sometimes they just want to be dead, to escape from the pain that they feel. But those are all *symptoms*, not the cause. Everyone needs purpose, direction and love.

'When Simon and a gang of other lads were taken to a YMCA camp, Eurocross, the camp organisers didn't know what had hit them. From the clothing they were wearing, they looked tough, and people expected trouble; but they were dead soft. I called them 'my little treasures'. Simon was was on remand at that time – I got the police to release him into my custody.

'There was a group of black lads there from Bradford, and I could see Simon's mates eyeing them up; it looked at though there was going to be trouble. But we countered the possibility of racial violence by introducing the two gangs to each other, and they ended up as great friends – they even went disco-dancing together.

'It is not just skinheads, though; some of the older people in Harrogate have the view that coloured people are not quite so good really. That's just ignorance of other cultures.'

Occasionally, Rosie worked specifically with the girls. One girl she remembers is Jenny, who now works as a care assistant at a home for mentally handicapped people. 'Jenny asked me recently, "Was I really awful when I was about fifteen or sixteen?" I said, "Jenny, you were absolutely foul!" She once picked her boy friend up and threw him through a full-length mirror! But I can remember thinking that there was something there, and that one day she would come through; so I just carried on loving her.

'I phoned the centre one day and Jenny answered the phone. I could hear her saying, "It's the bloody Fuhrer on the phone!" So, on her eighteenth birthday, I sent her some flowers with a card: "From the Fuhrer."

Though Rosie has occasionally persuaded young people to go to church with her, it has been the usual uphill struggle. The church members feel uncomfortable. They are generally not happy to see what they believe to be a bunch of useless layabouts on their pews.

'But they are not layabouts, they are just kids, and they are not all from bad homes. Sometimes they come from what we would call "Nice" homes. The only way they'll be right is for the Jesus-shaped hole to be filled by Jesus. You can patch things, and you can make life a little better for them; you can be very useful going to court with them – I've prayed in some funny places, but I never thought that I'd be praying on the steps outside the court – but in the end it is Jesus they need.'

Though Rosie received substantial help in her work, as her team strived to help the young people whom no one else wanted to know, the final responsibility was always hers. Though, as co-ordinator, she tried to delegate responsibilities to other helpers, they kept coming back to her. There were problems with the management committee, too.

'In 1986, God told me quite clearly that I had to leave the project. I had a real peace about it.' She left on July 30th and went off on holiday. She had booked Harrogate Conference Centre, at a cost of £2,500, for a Saturday in November, believing that God was calling her to bring Christians in Harrogate together 'to lift the name of Jesus on high'. The Festival of Praise was to feature an orchestra, choir, dance and drama group drawn from members of thirty or forty local churches.

In retrospect, Rosie can see God's timing clearly in the choice of departure date. While on holiday, she nearly died from a respiratory complaint on a Spanish campsite where no doctor was available; a few days later, her daughter was seriously assaulted; other members of the family were ill or injured; and her handbag was stolen – with money, passports, credit cards and travellers' cheques in it. The holiday was a disaster.

Rosie is convinced that it was the devil's work to distract her from the Festival of Praise. She feels that, if she had not left the drop-in project at the time she did, the pressure of organizing both the project *and* the event, on top of the holiday experiences, would have been too overwhelming for her to have done either successfully. The Festival was an enormous success. But, without Rosie, the drop-in centre floundered and eventually closed.

'I was sad about it, but nothing – apart from God – is for ever. Obedience to *his* will was more important than any youth project. Sometimes I look back and think, "Ooh dear, it's gone. Were we right in what we did!" Then I talk to people who say, "Remember what came out of the project, and the people who went through it who were changed." '

Rosie is now becoming involved with the local British Youth for Christ. After a year off, she is exploring ways to re-open the drop-in centre with a less bureaucratic structure: 'I really want to do something with frontier kids, because I really miss them! Mind you, it has to be exactly what God wants, not just a crazy idea of mine . . .'

8

A stitch in time

Tim Barker – Castleford

'I haven't done anything wrong!' exclaimed the prisoner, perched on his bed in the narrow cell. 'Who are you to interfere with my way of life?' Probation officer Tim Barker listened in disgust to the ranting man who had committed horrific sexual offences against a ten-year-old girl: 'When I get out, I'm going to do it again!'

Tim was so angry that he raged out, slammed the cell door, and stormed back to his office. 'Lord,' he cried out, 'how can I love a man like that? A man who is going to leave this prison and commit other offences.'

Several years later, Tim smiles at the recollection. 'As sure as I'm sitting here today, I heard the Lord say to me, "You're not going to love him, but I can love him through you. You may have given up on this man, but I haven't. Now, get yourself back in that cell!"

'I went back.

'I don't know the conclusion to that story, because the prisoner has not yet been released; but I know of another sex-offender, Martin, who showed signs that he wanted to do something about his life. Martin was a classic failure. Poor lad, he couldn't even commit crime successfully. He began to read John's Gospel, and he completed a Bible study correspondence course. As he was doing that, the Lord just seemed to meet him.

He was serving his third ten-year sentence, and had *always* offended within days of being released, but we were able to find him a place in a Christian home. Contact was established before he was released, a good relationship developed, Martin moved out there and he has been on the straight and narrow for a considerable time. The Lord loves a good challenge!'

The roots of Martin's sexual offences were laid down in his own childhood. He himself was sexually abused as a child. As Martin grew older, he developed an intimate relationship with a girl; she claimed that he had raped her, and he received his first prison sentence. Those problems had never been resolved, and the combination of rebellion against her and resentment against the parents who had abused him needed to be brought to the surface, with gentle support from Tim, so that they could be dealt with, and healing could take place.

Tim first wanted to join the probation service while he was still at school. His parents were Warden and Matron of a probation home in Kent, and they gave him his first contact with the service, though he himself was actually at a boarding school in Scotland. Tim was a contemporary of Prince Charles: 'We were in the same class for certain subjects. He showed an interest in the Christian Union which I helped to set up.'

Tim's housemaster suggested that it would be preferable for him to get some experience of life before getting into a training situation, so he joined the Merchant Navy.

'Suddenly finding myself on board a tanker, I came across many things that I had not experienced at public school!' he says. 'I'm indebted. With hindsight, it was a very wise decision – though, at the time, it was a bit hairy!'

After two years with Shell Tankers, Tim moved on to get some shop-floor experience in cost and works accountancy, before obtaining a Certificate of Qualification in Social Work (CQSW) from Leeds Univeristy. This is the minimum qualification to become a probation officer.

He first worked for what was then the Bradford Probation Office, covering a bed-sitter area that had once been very prosperous but had gradually become run down. Part of Tim's time was spent as Liaison Officer with a drug unit, operating in the twilight worlds of both drug offenders and psychiatric patients.

Probation is often seen, erroneously, as a way of punishing offenders without sending them to prison. It is true that, in the late 1980's, there has been a shift in emphasis: the glut of offenders in custodial care – 51,000 – has overloaded the prison and probationary services to an extent that makes rehabilitation difficult. To some extent, then, being on probation is a form of punishment; but it is much more than that.

Probation seeks to enable offenders to remain in the community, whilst encouraging them to examine his/her own behaviour with a view to making changes. There are many ways of achieving this, ranging from one-to-one interviews (usually at least one per week), assessment groups (a series of perhaps six sessions), drop-in centres, and day centres where they can be taught basic skills. There is regular contact with the probation officer, and it is *not* cosy. When a young probationer attends, he/she knows that they are going to have a hard time; they will have to confront some very difficult areas of change.

'There are role-plays and prayer exercises where they have to assess themselves,' says Tim. 'A lot depends on the offender's level of articulation, but these are designed to highlight to us the offender's feelings, how he sees the problem, and what he is going to do about it. We are a listening ear, pushing back to him what we feel that he is saying, and getting him to work through it.'

Sometimes, young offenders give grúdging one-word answers. Then it is common to put them into a group situation, where verbal communication is not the only means of expression. They might play the board game *Colditz*, which can reveal a lot about what the individual is trying – or failing – to communicate. This may, for example, help an offender to realize that he is perceived as very aggressive, something he may never have understood before.

'Sometimes we do non-verbal communication exercises, where people don't talk at all. They are simply told that they can get up, move around, move other people around, or stay where they are. You soon start to see leaders emerge, and you see the people who become aggressive if they can't get their own way. We have these techniques which enable us to get beneath the limited verbal skills of the offenders. Drama therapy, too, is tremendously useful, enabling them to say things that they would not normally be able to express.

'Young people often become aggressive out of frustration at being unable to express themselves. We need to help them to understand what is happening, and that there are other ways of demonstrating their feelings. We might role-play a situation leading up to someone smashing a bus shelter window, then stop the role play at that point, and ask them what alternatives were available.'

Tim has often used Scripture Union filmstrips such as *In the Bin* or *Number One* as discussion-starters in group sessions. One of the role-plays he finds particularly successful is to have the young offenders act out a sentencing situation such as they might experience in a court room: 'It is very useful to see how they would sentence people for the offence that they have themselves committed!' It is an exercise that would work, too, in a conventional youth club situation, to make young people think about the issues of crime and violence.

Tim is also a volunteer worker at a church-sponsored club, and he finds that his probation service background gives him an original slant on youth club work: 'I think that in a traditional youth club, where you play table-tennis or listen to noisy records in smoke-filled rooms, a tremendous amount of useful work can be done by someone who simply has time *to sit down and listen*. So many young people *desperately* need someone to show sufficient interest in them to sit and listen. Doing that can give them back a lot of the self-confidence and self-importance that has been eroded by their oppressive social circumstances.' Such an approach could probably help to reduce the number of young people who pass into the care of the probation service each year.

While Tim was working with drug abusers as Probation Liaison Officer at Waddiloves Hospital, he found that having all the offenders together in one group was the exact opposite of what was needed. Being together was causing them to become obsessed with drug use to the exclusion of anything and everything else. The solution was to mix the drug abusers with mentally disturbed offenders. The drug users were able to *identify* with the psychiatric cases – one of whom was addicted to cough mixture, while another was prone to viciously biting people – in a way which challenged their own attitudes to drugs.

Tim worked closely with the nursing staff in this setting. He ran group sessions one half-day per week, as well as seeing patients on a one-to-one basis. It was not unusual to be called out in the middle of the night.

'I did group work there relating to specific topics. Perhaps relationships, coping in a bed-sit, or DHSS regulations. This helped us to assess individuals during treatment, and to prepare them for transfer into the local community. People progressed from being in-patients to being day-patients, and then out-patients, as they learned to cope gradually.

'One person had undergone a sex-change, and needed a lot of basic teaching on how to cope as a female. She had served a jail sentence and was released on parole, on condition that she attended Waddiloves Hospital. For me, the whole business of looking at the issue of sex-change from a Christian viewpoint caused tremendous problems. I had to cope with something I didn't agree with, in a situation where I was expected to be of constructive help. Nor was it a one-off situation. I couldn't condone it, but I believe that the Lord shows compassion to people. I tried to do the same, seeking to be a witness to my lifestyle, without approving of their actions.'

Tim is constantly in the position of having to counsel young offenders who are considering abortions. There, too, his responsibility as a probation officer is to help them to make up their own minds: 'Putting my head in the sand and saying, 'It's unchristian,' doesn't help people to make their own decisions.'

Sometimes the decision is not the one Tim agrees with, but he has to see the situation through to the stage of passing the pregnant offender on to a doctor: 'But we will have spent many hours looking at all the options. Whereas it is relatively straightforward to make the arrangements for an abortion to take place, quite frequently it is not till many years later that the guilt feelings come to the surface – perhaps when the girl gets married and thinks of starting a family, but is still carrying the burden bf the past. I have to help people to see the ramifications of their decisions, otherwise I'm contributing to detrimental effects later on.

'I've never felt that my Christian faith has prevented me from completing a task – or inhibited me in a task – within the probation service. The service originally began with a concern of the Police Commissioners in London, but I think we have gone a long way away from the original emphasis. Christians coming into the service today *can* feel at odds. I count it a privilege to be helping to mould new people coming into the service.

'The majority of my clients have known exactly where I stand as a Christian. They have known that I cannot condone any behaviour that is not in line with the Christian faith. They have also known that, having said that, I will do all that I can to help them in terms of their basic and rightful needs, and offer whatever support I can in their situations.'

Tim finds that many people believe young offenders will 'grow out of' crime as soon as they meet a member of the opposite sex and fall in love. That is often true, but it does not mean that they will grow out of problems. He has to prepare young offenders for life, and settling down with a partner often brings along a lot of new problems and multiplies the old ones. The probation officer needs to work on these situations, otherwise this can be a source of potential problems for the future.

A lot of the problems and growing pains of the young people with whom Tim works stem from their home environment. It has been too easy, Tim feels, for parents to opt out of their responsibilities. A combination of apathy and disorganization has led to a lack of discipline. A lot of difficulties arise from young people rushing – or being rushed – into marraige, and having families too quickly, before they have had time to cope with their own growing pains.

For several years in the early 1980's, Tim worked at Wakefield Prison – one of Britain's top security prisons, holding 700 men, half of whom were serving life sentences. Many had committed offences against children; others were terrorists, rapists, murderers and violent offenders. Security was paramount, and it was difficult to find the space for rehabilitation work. Statistics show that custodial sentences alone do not stop offenders from returning to violence and crime when they are released. Eighty per cent will re-offend.

Though the majority of the prisoners were aged over twenty-one, some were younger, and even the older prisoners had serious problems which related back to experiences in their youth. Those with life sentences were at Wakefield at the beginning of their term, and the emphasis for the first three years was on assessment. Reports made by Tim and his colleagues, in addition to reports made by others in the prison service, were forwarded to the Home Office to be used as a basis to determine a date for the first review of each offender's case.

'My work there was mainly on a one-to-one basis, often helping the prisoners to come to terms with the indeterminate nature of their sentences, to cope with the very real possibility of the breakdown of their marriage, and to get to grips with the prison way of life. I was able to organize some group work, too – a pre-release course for those about to be freed, a basic social skills course, and an alcohol education course.'

There were some very dangerous and very disturbed people in the prison. Though the younger ones were about to spend the 'best years of their lives' behind bars, Tim was amazed at how philosophical they were about their sentences. The biggest problems, he found, were working with child-molesters and sexual offenders; though that is a problem whether the offender is in prison or simply on probation.

'I'm currently working with a lad named Pip, who is a sex offender. Pip knows that, when he comes to see me, he is going to have to look carefully – and, at times, very painfully – at his behaviour, and how it needs to change. He will be expected to complete exercises that will highlight his behaviour. The exercises examine his motivation – to find out what excites him, and what causes him to commit offences against, in this case, young boys.

'Often the exercises point back to his own experiences as a child. Statistics indicate that sex offenders have often been sexually abused themselves as a child, so I have to persuade them to talk about what they suffered when, perhaps, for a number of years they have not wanted to face up to it, in order to put what they are doing themselves into perspective. We have to correct their pattern of behaviour, so that they can express themselves in a way acceptable to society.

'Sometimes, the root problem lies in a failure to see girls and women as individuals in themselves; they are seen only as objects of sexual gratification. Sometimes, willing partners cry off at the last moment, and that kind of offence must be treated differently from one where a man has methodically sought out a girl and committed a cold, calculated rape; but both instance an inadequacy and inability to form meaningful, lasting relationships.

In cases where a person's sex drive is particularly strong, the solution may be medical treatment to reduce it, and Tim recalls a sexual offender at Waddiloves who was in this situation. His sex drive was chemically reduced, he married and had a normal relationship with his wife – there was no re-offence. 'While I have some understanding of people's outraged reactions to the crime of rape,' says Tim, 'we need to consider each offence as an individual case.'

Tim has also worked in a probation hostel for twenty-five single 17–19 year olds, many of whom lived there as a condition of their probation order. Typically, the offenders lived there for twelve months, usually where there were domestic problems which made it unwise for them to be allowed to serve out their probation at their parental home. Tim worked mainly on a one-to-one basis with these offenders, whose crimes were normally minor offences such as theft, burglary or stealing cars.

One lad, Garth, had a problem relating to his mother, though the initial symptoms suggested that the problem lay in the relationship with his father. Garth felt that his mother had never really wanted him, and that he was rejected by his brothers and sisters, who always seemed to be better treated than himself. Tim eventually brought mother and son together in the hostel, to get Garth to bring his fears out into the open, and to get the mother's reaction. She responded remarkably well, and a reconciliation was achieved.

In his present post as Senior Probation Officer in Castleford, West Yorkshire, Tim is responsible for a team of seven probation officers, a probation assistant, five clerical staff, two cleaners, and about twenty volunteers. 'Anyone can apply to be a volunteer in their own area, he emphasizes. 'There is a desperate need, and the range of work is quite extensive.' Applicants should write to their local probation office in the first instance.

His role is mainly leading and co-ordinating; though he is involved, too, in a project which is working on the problem of accommodation for single people on probation. There is a desperate need for accommodation for single people in West Yorkshire. Castleford is a very parochial area; people live and die there only rarely venturing out of the town. To place young offenders in need of accommodation, say, in the excellent homeless person's hostel in Leeds, would be akin to exiling them on the far side of the globe. It would cause them stress, anxiety and suffering to be separated from their native environment.

Together with local clergy, Tim's team is establishing a homelessness project in Castleford. The local churches are involved in contributing to a clothing store, to help the families of offenders who are on a tight budget and are hard hit by government changes in DHSS special grants regulations. 'It's great to be able to work with local Christians. It's the first time that I've been able to do that as a probation officer in the local community.

'When Adullam Homes, a Christian housing association based in Birmingham ('Adullam' is the cave where David hid from Saul when he was homeless), wrote to a colleague of mine wanting to explore the possibility of a project in West Yorkshire, those who don't understand would say it was a coincidence – but I believe it was the Lord's doing.

'I contacted their development officer and progressed it for them. We will get the first four-bedroomed home very shortly. The project will include some teaching, helping young people to acquire the social skills to move into a home of their own.'

Tim's father was once the full-time Frontier Youth Trust worker in the Yorkshire region, and he also helped to establish FYT work in the Humberside region. Tim is following the family tradition. He sits on the local FYT committee, helps with training events, and is involved with church youth club work. He knows the problems of trying to run such a club when the older church members seem more concerned with the risk of damage to the church building!

'There are a lot of depersonalising situations today,' Tim says of the youth situation as he sees it. 'They erode the sparkle, the adventure and the enthusiasm from life. There's a loss of appetite for the sanctity of life itself. It has been replaced by frustration, and a need to be heard, which contributes to much of the hooliganism and football violence that takes place. We, as Christians, need to get alongside young people and give them some self-confidence, treating them as adults whose opinions matter.'

9

No easy road

Rosey Kelly – Holywood

Rosey Kelly's work at The Hob drop-in centre brings her into constant contact with young people who lack self-confidence and suffer from the depersonalising effects of a life without meaning and direction.

The Hob is based in the small town of Holywood, a twenty-minute bus ride from the centre of Belfast. Before taking up her post there, Rosey spent seven years as a teacher in a secondary school on the outskirts of Belfast. During that time she also helped as a volunteer at a local youth club attached to her church.

'I was surprised, at first, that I could actually *talk* to the young people in the club,' she says. 'I got along with them quite easily on a superficial level. The more involved I got, the more I enjoyed it. A year after I started, the leader dropped out and there was no one to take over, so a friend and I shared the leadership role.

'With a team of eight or nine committed helpers, the club ticked over for a few more years. It was an open youth club, attracting both the children of the middle-class church members, and an element from the nearby Whiteabbey village who were on the other side of the tracks.'

These local young people from unchurched backgrounds were a revelation to Rosey. She began to learn about the culture of young people who were not from grammar schools, or middle-class families. In common with the young people described in earlier chapters of this book, their backgrounds were deprived, and they would not normally go anywhere near a church.

Rosey warmed to these young people, and enjoyed being with them.

After attending a youth leader's course, she began to consider the *real* needs of the local young people. Her club was operating in a large church hall with plenty of space, but nowhere comfortable to sit down, chat and be informal. She began to see a need for a place not given over to a whirlwind of activity, and was surprised to discover that a group of Christians in Holywood on the other side of Belfast were working towards establishing a local drop-in centre, very much in that mould. These Christians had seen that there was nothing on offer in the area for young people who were not from a grammar school or church background. Though such people were a minority in affluent Holywood, they could be seen hanging around on street corners with limitless potential for getting into serious trouble. Rosey successfully applied for the job of youth worker at the drop-in centre.

The fund-raising and design of the centre had been finalized before Rosey took up office. The premises include a comfortable coffee bar on the ground floor, and a club room with darts, pool, computing, board games and small crafts facilities on the first floor. Toilets, and a small office take up the little remaining space. The drop-in centre, which is named the Hob, has contact with other youth clubs in the area, and also with youth organizations associated with several of the local churches. The Hob runs a programme which is complementary to all these other groups.

There are two main drop-in evenings, Tuesday and Thursday, from 8.00 to 11.00 pm. Anyone from the age of fifteen through to early twenties can come and go as they please within those times, and can make full use of the facilities offered. Often, they are content simply to sit and talk. On three afternoons, the same facilities are available for the use of unemployed young people.

From time to time, one of these afternoons is given over to something more specific; perhaps an action learning course, teaching life skills. Such a course might consider for example, how to go about applying for a job, using video tapes and mock phone calls; developing skills in photography or film-making; visiting community workshops; or any of a wide variety of other activities. Typically, only the bare bones of the course would be planned in advance, allowing the young people to give input to the course contents. In 1986, three such courses were run with varying degrees of success, all with a deliberately small number of participants, to allow for individual attention. The most successful began with a dozen participants and finished with four or five, as the participants took what they needed then dropped out. The Hob regularly works with smaller numbers than would a youth club.

The centre sometimes opens on additional evenings and afternoons to cater for specialist sessions such as a guitar course, a baking night, printing, etc. These are usually fairly short-lived: 'The interest and commitment of the young people – with a few exceptions – is difficult to maintain. That's partly due to Holywood being generally an affluent area with a comparatively low unemployment rate. The young people who attend the drop-in centre are – by and large – the least highly motivated, and the least successful. They are the ones who find it the most difficult to make a mark for themselves in any system. To expect people like that to come up with ideas or initiatives – or have the commitment to see things through – is perhaps unrealistic,' Rosey explains.

Rural Holywood is a dormitory town for office workers commuting the few miles into Belfast. Private developments and small council estates sit to the sides of the main street of what is very much a one-horse town. Holywood has a minority (perhaps thirty to forty per cent) Catholic population, though, to date, there has never been any major sectarian trouble in the town itself. There are many mixed marriages and mixed friendships. The local grammar school has a high proportion of Catholic pupils, compared with many other State grammar schools, who mix well with the Protestants.

'In my mind, though, there is always a question mark. If you scratched the surface of a mixed friendship, would the friendship be more important than the religious roots? I don't know the answer, and I imagine that it varies. But every so often, the pro-loyalist Protestant element among the young people who frequent The Hob seeks to dominate. We stand very strongly against that.'

The sectarian divide, on the surface, is a religious issue – a division between the Catholic and Protestant church traditions – but often this division seems to be used merely as an excuse to recruit for political ends. Many of the young people in Northern Ireland have relatives who are practising Christians, from whom they have been able to gain a more realistic picture of what the Christian faith is *really* about. There is, however, still much confusion in their minds – much of it put there by so-called Christian leaders:

'There are quite a few people in Northern Ireland, at various levels, who distort religion for political reasons,' says Rosey. 'They quote from the Bible to support what they have to say. Clichés, with out-of-context Bible texts attached, are what stick in the minds of the young people. It is not easy to find convincing arguments to show why such views are not *really* what the Bible teaches.'

In 1985, a loyalist flute band formed in the Holywood area, and since then it has been attracting young people from The Hob. 'Whatever the intentions of those who formed the band, it certainly seems to have aggravated sectarian unrest,' says Rosey. 'The young people come away from band practices stirred up, and full of all manner of jargon. Their motivation for going stems partly from a sense of wanting to *belong* to something, and partly because it is something in which they can *involve* themselves.

'Earlier this year, two young men well known to us through the club got themselves drawn into the fringes of paramilitary activity. They were involved in the armed hijacking of a lorry, with sectarian motives. Once they get involved, it's very difficult to extricate themselves,' says Rosey, echoing Noel Hunter's experiences in the Falls Road area.

Holywood is a garrison town. The local police station is surrounded by a formidable fence, and there are restrictions on how close to the station drivers can park their cars, for fear of car bombing. The largest army barracks in Northern Ireland is just outside Holywood. Soldiers frequent several local pubs at weekends, and fights are not uncommon. If there were no soldiers and no sectarian issue, Rosey believes, there would still be fights – because the offenders would find other reasons to justify the expression of their aggression. A number of The Hob's 'regulars' have been involved in petty theft and shop-breaking. Some have caused damage to parked cars by climbing up and walking over the roofs while drunk. Driving offences, such as taking and driving away, and riding motorbikes without tax or insurance, are common. Sectarian fighting seems to be really just another example of the young people's undisciplined lifestyle and lawlessness.

Often there is no *obvious* antagonism; but when feelings are stirred up, one faction will attempt to aggravate the other – perhaps by pinning up their flags on The Hob's walls, or by painting slogans. The atmosphere of intimidation is seldom absent. Some of the lads like to think of themselves as 'hard men'; and some of the 'regulars', afraid that full-blooded sectarian violence will erupt, have stopped coming.

In Spring 1987, the centre was invited by another youth club to take part in a competition based on the TV show *Blind Date*. Rosey took a minibus-load of young people from both Protestant and Catholic backgrounds. On the way, a small group began to drum their feet and to sing loyalist songs. On arrival, the event turned out to be something of an anti-climax, so some of the young people sneaked off for a few drinks. As a result, the singing on the return journey was louder and more boisterous. Unknown to Rosey and her fellow leaders, one girl in particular was singled out for sectarian insult, and was kicked just after getting off the bus.

'It was possibly a case of personal antagonism, with the sectarian differences used as an excuse. We had a hoo-ha about the incident after we found out, though several members said that it hadn't happened in the centre, so what had it to do with me? But the parents of the girl who had been kicked, and those of another girl who had been insulted, complained to me about the incident being allowed to happen on our trip.'

The second major problem facing the young people of Holywood is the familiar one of unemployment; but, this time, the problem presents a more unusual face. The unemployment rate is only in the region of five to ten per cent. For those few who *are* unemployed, their minority status highlights their sense of despair and rejection. It is one thing to be unemployed in an area where unemployment is the norm – on parts of Merseyside for example – and quite another to have no job when all one's peer group are seen to be doing something useful and financially rewarding. The stigma is greater, too.

It is not easy to look for work without travelling quite a distance. There are no manufacturing companies in the Holywood area. Though agricultural work is sometimes available, the young people are 'townies' with family backgrounds in factories, not fields. It would be a brave young man indeed who made the leap into farm work, though some have been out into the nearby countryside as volunteers doing conservative work. Not many have done it, but those who have seem to have enjoyed the change of pace.

For the young people still without jobs, the future looks bleak . . .

'Someone approached me last year to see if we had half a dozen young people whom he could take on for a week's labouring work, at a shopping complex,' says Rosey. 'He arranged to sort out all the problems that the young people would have in coming off the dole just for a week, and the work went ahead. There were two bosses – the one who arranged the work initially,

124

and another who was actually on the site. They told the six lads who went that there was a strong possibility that at least one of them would be taken on permanently, if they did a good job. Some of them really slogged away, though others wasted time and gave a poor impression of the whole group.

'The six were all given a second week's work, and they came into The Hob, bubbling about how much they had been paid. The next day, they came in and said that they had suddenly been paid off. They were effing and blinding and cursing because one of the bosses had not been entirely satisfied. He had seen something of the messing about and had tarred them all with the same brush. They were up one minute, and down again the next. The promises had come to nothing. They felt abused, and it was some considerable time before it all subsided.'

Typically, Rosey has about ten to a dozen unemployed young people using The Hob regularly. Others are in and out of work, and use the premises on an occasional basis. In all, unemployed young people constitute about a fifth of the regular users, but they are the most disadvantaged, particularly when it comes to trying to find money for housing.

To buy property in rural Holywood is expensive compared with most areas of Belfast. There is a great demand for housing in Holywood from people who want to move further away from the troubles, and the competition keeps the prices high. The small stretch of countryside between Belfast and Holywood works wonders, psychologically, in establishing a sense of distance, while the town is still sufficiently close to make commuting an easy matter.

"There are only two main council estates, so the choice is limited, and the competition fierce, for council accommodation. People have to stay on the waiting list for quite a time – or move elsewhere. I know of young people who have just got married, or had children, who *have* been able to secure council tenancies. There are also a few cases where couples have had the determination to find and hold down jobs, have stuck at it, planned ahead, saved some money – with help from their parents – and been able to start married life in a small place of their own. But they are very much a minority amongst the young people who come to The Hob. There is very little private sector accommodation to let in the area.'

Not all the relationships are sanctified by marriage. Several couples who use the drop-in centre live together, and have children, without any intention of ever walking down the aisle together. Sadly, others *have* married, but have since split up and divorced. Christian moral values in the area of sexual ethics are communicated to the young people in informal discussions. A common response is the assertion that Chritianity equals middle-class – that it is 'different' for Christian couples, because Christians have more money!

'They don't accept very easily any ideas that we have about how they ought to live their lives. Just because something is "Christian" doesn't give it any special virtue in their eyes,' says Rosey. 'There is no way that we can – or would want to – ram our opinions down their throats. They know that we accept them as they are, for the most part; only when something affects the life of The Hob – such as the sectarian problem – would we take a firm stand.'

Unmarried mothers with small children call in from time to time. The wife of one of Rosey's fellow workers has connections with a local mums-and-toddlers group to which some of them go. Rosey has considered running a similar group as part of the centre's programme, though the premises are not really suitable; there is, for example, no storage space for toys. Renovations in the coffee bar will result in new soft seating, and a carpeted area, which might make it more suited to young children, and it is possible that a small-scale activity for young mothers will eventually be introduced. The contacts are there, and the opportunity exists to explore some of the needs of such a group. Many of the single-parent families are themselves from single-parent homes. It is the exception rather than the rule for one of Rosey's clients to come from a stable two-parent home. Some of the young people's behaviour obviously stems from that instability.

About a third as many girls as men attend The Hob, but there have been enough strong female 'characters' to hold their own – for example, by beating the men at such traditional male pastimes as pool and darts. Sexual stereotypes are broken down, too, on baking night, when some of the male members have shown themselves to be adept cooks. Rosey has considered outreach work to contact other girls, to redress the balance of the sexes, and to discover their special needs which the centre may be able to meet. An influx of new girls often coincides with the availability of unattached males at The Hob, so there is clearly an element of the centre being used as a dating agency. If that attraction disappears, the new girls disappear too – unless they have been coming long enough to feel a part of the scene.

There are three full-time staff at The Hob, along with eight or nine dependable volunteers from local churches. Rosey herself has a teaching qualification which, until 1987, was recognized as a suitable qualification for professional youth work. Rosey disputes whether this was ever fair – 'teaching and youth work are very different animals.' She completed a foundation course in youth work, prior to starting work at the centre, with additional post-foundation modules in Working with Girls and Basic Canoeing – even though the centre has no canoes of its own, nor anywhere they could be stored. Three of the other leaders have completed the foundation course, and one has completed the Mountain Leadership module.

'He could take young people walking and camping, though we don't often do very much of that – not as much as we would like – partly because of indifference on the part of the regular users. Though a certain amount of camping has been done, it's never been possible to get together an ongoing programme, which is disappointing. We have used the facilities at the YMCA in Bangor, although we have had to pay for them. Planning and co-ordination are a headache.

'There is inevitably a minor drink problem at the Hob, and we occasionally get soft drugs being used, too, though usually no worse than in many youth clubs. The problems caused by drink were illustrated recently during a camping trip to Scotland. We discussed the whole matter before we went away, and agreed on reasonable levels of alcohol consumptiion for the over-eighteens that would not have had a bad influence on the younger members. Promises were broken, and expectations were not met. The crucial issue was less to do with drinking than a failure to adhere to agreements.

'I'd like to see more training taking place, though perhaps with a slightly different angle from secular training organizations and agencies. It's a struggle to interpret the secular models for Christian use. FYT is one of the few bodies that is trying to work that out in different situations. We value the contact we have with FYT.'

Rosey is a member of the Northern Ireland FYT committee, and some of the thinking that is being done there is thinking that she and the team at the Hob are trying to thrash out. Working with Maurice Kinkead – FYT's Northern Ireland field officer – and others, Rosey is looking at issues which particularly need to be tackled, and for which training ought to be organized. (Maurice himself is currently working at The Bridge drop-in centre near to the heart of Belfast, just across the road from Ian Paisley's church hall.)

On various occasions, Rosey and her co-workers have sat around with young people informally studying the Bible, but only for short spells – it has never been possible to maintain the interest. That may be a key area that needs to be looked at.

'In the four years that The Hob has been running, we know of four or five young people who have become Christians, who have had some involvement here. By and large, once they have become Christians, either circumstances have taken them away, or they have chosen not to stay. Invariably, there has been some Christian influence in addition to The Hob that has led them to the point of commitment. There are other young people who come regularly and who go through stages of seeming to be very close to making a decision. We have had long conversations with them, and, they will defend Christianity in group discussions, but that is as far as they go,' says Rosey, sadly.

Christians from the local churches which were responsible for starting the drop-in centre continue to give prayer and financial support, but only a few are involved in a practical way. Rosey has become increasingly dissatisfied with traditional formats for church worship. She feels that church life is not 'on the same wavelength' as the anguished young people with whom she works: 'There is no real "sending community" of Christians who will give depth and breadth of support and develop a close understanding of what is going on here. Churches, so often, are just not aware of the growing pains of young people out on the streets.'

It is an all too familiar situation. The middle-class churches are seen by many young people as irrelevant; in their minds, that makes the death and resurrection of Jesus Christ irrelevant, too. Often, the social implications of the gospel have been lost, and evangelism limited to working with the young people who are regular church attenders, rather than those on the outside.

American preacher and sociologist Tony Campolo spoke with vigour on this problem at Greenbelt 1987: 'If we lose this generation of young people it will not be because we have made the gospel too hard, but because we have made it too easy. *Youth is made for heroism and not for pleasure.* I find it much easier to get someone to say "yes" to a Jesus who requires them to sell everything and to lay down their life in Christian service, than to get them to move from paganism to becoming a middle-class churchman. The latter is so boring it could interest no one, and the former is so interesting that it challenges everyone. If a young person says, "I've heard the call, what do you want me to do?" and all we say is, "Show up for church, be at the prayer meeting and witness at school," then we are undermining their enthusiasm!'

The style of radical discipleship that Campolo advocates is illustrated by the work of the nine projects encountered in the last nine chapters. The young people that Noel, Maureen, John, Willy, Martin, George,

Rosie, Tim and Rosey work with are, frankly, not very promising material with which to build a church for the twenty-first century. But look at what Jesus had to work with when he built the first-century church. James and John, the 'Sons of Thunder', sound like the equivalent of today's punks. In fact, the only one who really qualified to be a disciple was Judas.

Rosey's drop-in centre, like the other youth projects, doesn't run missions: 'It *is* a mission. The whole work is mission, both what we do and the issues with which we grapple. Our own lives and what we say about Christianity are a part of it, too, though we perhaps err on the side of saying too little in comparison with the traditional evangelical approach. 'The Hob is a refuge for those young people who have been alienated by modern society and, sadly, by the Church. The ordinary church format and music is a turn-off to the majority of today's youth, and it is doubtful in any case whether they would be accepted or want to be accepted – into such an unfamiliar environment.

'The young people here can see Christians – warts and all – and can see that you don't have to be someone special in order to become a Christian. When they go elsewhere and hear the gospel in a more familiar form, they can say, "Well, I've seen something of that being put into action."

'We don't think of our work as being short-term. We would be delighted if one, or a group, came to faith and decided to stay here, getting to work immediately, wrestling with us to work out – and to live out – what it is to be a follower of Christ in this situation. We long for that to happen, though maybe we'll never see it. We don't know what we *should* expect – but we are not discouraged. It's a long, slow process.'

Afterword

In the Frontiers of Youth Work

Michael Eastman

These nine people are good news to lost young people. They are typical of those whom God is using to make his good news a reality amongst the young outside the reach and beyond the understanding of most Christians and most churches. They are at the fore-front of one of the major missionary challenges confronting the Church.

Faith in the City, the report of the Archbishops' Commission on Urban Priority Areas, concluded:

> . . . there are sizeable groups of young people who are trapped in UPAs, who only gain attention when they become a threat, who are denied equality of opportunity and life chances and with whom the Churches have little or no contact. It is difficult to exaggerate how alienated these young people are: from adult ideas of how young people should behave; from their peers of different social classes; from agencies they think of an acting on adults' behalf and not usually in the interests of young people, eg from the police; from school; and from the churches.' (p. 315)

These are the 'failures' in our much vaunted 'enterprise culture'. The losers who live and grow up in the world in which they experience the harsh realities of life on the downside of our society. Martin Hardwidge and Tim Barker tell of **child abuse**, Maureen Davies, Willy Holland and Martin of **drugs and solvent abuse**. George Watson tells of **homelessness**, several, including Rosie Towers and Rosie Kelly talk of **crime**. AIDS, varied sexual orientation and gangs, are part of the picture. John Hutchison conveys the human consequences of whole scale **redevelopment** and its effects on every day living of **policies** argued over and decided by those in power.

The Youth Workers who tell their stories here live and work among these young people and experience the same realities. For twenty five years Frontier Youth Trust has been serving them. In 1955 a handful came together to share their experiences, largely of failure, and to seek to understand what God was showing them. This informal association grew, with a series of annual conferences and from it FYT was formed in 1964. The Trust has been linked with Scripture Union since 1966. In 1974 Scripture Union published *Go Down in the City*, telling the stories of nine frontier youth workers. It is an even tougher world to grow up in now than then. High levels of youth unemployment remain endemic in UPAs. Martin Hardwidge and Rosie Kelly witness to its corrosive effects.

Faith in the City notes that this

'. . . has disrupted the normal progression of development from home to school to job; and the time during which a young person is dependent on home and family has been extended. The prolonging of financial dependency creates problems both for parents and their children, who live in a youth culture which relies on an adequate income. But above all it has removed one of the main ways a young person has of valuing himself or herself. Many young people are extremely resilient and seem able to transcend their environment with hope in their hearts. Others have spoken to us of the hurt of watching young people grow through childhood to adolescence and beyond, and as they do so experiencing a transformation from the normal expectancy and hope of the young, through apparent resignation to the inner pain and anger of a life seemingly without hope.' (*Faith in the City*, p. 36)

It is this *low self image* with which frontier youth workers have to contend. Each of the nine stories touch on it. Tim Barker and Martin Hardwidge in particular note it. The young people they deal with are as much 'sinned against' as 'sinning'. Most have been let down by the adults in their lives – parents, teachers, the police, social workers, employers – and have been forced back on to their own inadequate resources. The streets are an unforgiving environment. The young become vulnerable to those who would exploit their youth. Their bodies have cash value. Drugs and alcohol are big business. The ideologies of hate find fertile ground. 'Alienation' – the making of people not least young people, to feel themselves to be 'outsiders' – is from a particular *order* that is felt unresponsive and uncaring.

'We have heard first hand of the fear of the destructive potential of young people. We have sensed the latent violence as we have walked along the streets; we have seen groups of young people – with nothing to do, nowhere to go and with nothing to lose:

"I wouldn't go out without a pair of scissors to defend me."

"If someone steps on your toe every day, and if they keep on doing it, you might do something drastic".' (*Faith in the City*, p. 36)

Violence is a variety of forms runs through these stories. Noel Hunter deals daily with it. Sometimes it's directed to property. Graffiti shouts where other forms of expression are blocked. Verbal abuse and physical attack are part of the backcloth as Maureen Davies knows. The violence which self-destructively turns inward slowly destroying the Creator's image in whom all are made can result in suicide as Martin Hardwidge knows first hand.

Frontier youth workers like these are bearers of hope. God has not given up on the young pushed out and shoved under in our society. The projects in which they are involved are gospel signs. They are like fields bought in enemy territory as a sign that God hasn't abandoned these situations (see Jeremiah 32). Other Christians might think them crazy to invest their lives in unpromising and unresponsive young people. These youth workers have taken Christ's first sermon as seriously as his last. Our Lord calls his people to discipline all nations and to make God's good news known to the poor and dispossessed (See Luke 4:18, 19; Matthew 28:19, 20).

God has called a wide variety of people to this ministry. Some are full time professionally trained youth workers, like Maureen, or teachers, like Rosie Kelly. Tim Barker and George Watson are trained social workers. Many work voluntarily, part-time. Others use their home, as Rosie Towers has done.

The situation and styles of work are also varied. Standard solutions don't apply. Some projects are *Centre based* – places where young people go with a range of activities and programmes available. The Hob, the Shewsie, St Helen's YWCA, Noel Hunters' Mission Hall in the Falls Road are of this kind. These can be under the auspices of a church or Christian agency. Others work as Christians in Local Authority Clubs.

Some go where the young people are to be found in pubs, cafes, amusement arcades, shopping precincts, the streets and street corners of our cities and featureless housing estates. Others, such as the Coke Hole, meet with young people at the crisis points in their lives, unemployed, into drugs, without shelter, in trouble of all kinds.

Christ's way is their example. They express God's heart and mind in person, as well as teach and explain who God is and what he requires. Presence precedes proclamation. George Watson makes this clear. Incarnation is at the heart of effective frontier mission. Rosie Towers knows it's a costly business. There's sheer wear-and-tear on time and energy. Noel Hunter notes the demands on family life, especially on ones own children. He also knows the approach and misunderstanding of other Christians. The lack at times of support from the Church is part of George's experience. Those who work with young people at risk arc themselves at risk. Tim Barker speaks of the tensions he faces and Maureen knows what it is like to live in a hostile environment. Each experiences something of the way of the Cross.

Some like those at the Shewsie and St Helens YWCA are local people, who themselves first learnt of Christ through frontier youth work. Many are not. As with John Hutchinson, they came to faith in contexts which if not geographicaly distant are culturally remote from the situations in which they now serve. They undertake the same journey as any missionary who leaves her or his own country and culture and is sent on God's mission to another context.

Young people, as Rosie Tower demonstrates, cannot

be loved at a distance. The initial step is to relocate, set up home, put down roots in the community to which you are sent. It's easier to cross continents than, like Willy Holland, move five miles into town and live the other side of the tracks. The language, customs and lifestyle of the new culture have to be learnt the hard way. It takes time to be accepted, known and trusted. Young people who have been let down by every adult they have known will test you to destruction, to find too, your breaking point. Maureen Davies learned this the hard way. Your own values may clash with those whom you seek to serve. This calls for tough, self-examination as Tim, Maureen and Rosey Kelly have found out. We are challenged to ask whether our values spring from seeking to follow Jesus or are part of our background and upbringing which get in the way of making Jesus known.

The *pastoral* needs are often overwhelming. George found that one young woman could take up most of one's time, and there were another sixty situations to be dealt with. No one can do everything. Sharp choices of priority are thrust upon the team. But what in this community or locality gives rise to these casualties? John Hutchison shows that an understanding of the *social* context is necessary. If people are the victims of the actions and decisions of others outside the area, if monstrous high rise flats or inadequate schools cause the problems how do we bring effective pressure to bear on the decision makers? How can we best be *advocates* for those without a voice and without access to those in power? George and John wrestle with these questions.

What about the **Church**? If the existing congregations don't fit the neighbourhood and only welcome the young on their terms how are frontier young people to be discipled? Can new forms of the church be developed? Noel faces this, as does Rosey Kelly. What about the Christian Faith? What is 'Good News for the poor'? How is the Bible to be understood and shared amongst those who don't or can't read? What does God's Kingdom of 'Justice, Shalom and Joy' look like in practice amongst these young people in this place? What are the 'principalities and powers' that hold communities in prison. How are they to be challenged and broken?

These are a daunting range of questions and experiences which don't need to be faced by comfortable Christians in comfortable churches in comfortable Britain. Frontier Youth Trust provides a context in which they can be worked at. Disturbing Christian voices have been raised from the frontier youth scene challenging the complacency and small mindedness of the churches.

There is much to be learnt from those whom God has called to work with him behind the enemy lines.

First God takes up and uses a wide variety of people in frontier ministry. Whilst professional training helps, without tough, unsentimental love in action relationships will not be built. Openness to the vulnerability of others, the willingness to be hurt, to listen, and to spend time, determined commitment, acceptance and non-judgemental attitudes are needed. This requires a down-to-earth spirituality. Those who give themselves to others who have little or nothing going for them experience more of God's presence and person. There is no resurrection without crucifixion. Prayer and faith is tested and deepened. Those who minister are changed.

Second, there are no quick, easy solutions. Places like the Shewsy and Coke Hole have been sustained over many years. This kind of stability and long term involvement tells its own story. It takes time to nurture the next generation of leadership, especially when working with young people at a vulnerable and transitional period of their lives. Teams are important. They model the message. Lifestyle tells the story before words are understood.

Partnership with others of goodwill is important. Those involved with the casualties of our society earn the right to question the causes. They act as a conscience and provide a channel. Public and charitable money needs effective means to achieve desirable ends. The very existence of such projects show that something can be done. Christians are thereby salt and light They find also that God is at work beyond the Church. The Spirit is not limited. Those who support and become drawn into such projects are touched by Christ.

Training helps. A great deal has been learnt the hard way by those engaged in frontier work over the last thirty or more years. This experience can be, must be, passed on. On the job training is best, learning in doing with time for reflection on what has been experienced is the most effective. There are skills in relating to and working with others. Training can develop and sharpen them. Discipling young frontier Christians, understanding and sharing the Christian faith, learning how to work with groups, and how to work across cultures are the staple diet of FYT training courses. Learning how to understand, analyse, assess and plan is also necessary. There is a great deal of knowledge common to those who work with young people upon which Christian frontier workers can draw.

Frontier youth work and youth workers need support. Understanding, sympathetic and informed pray-ers, places and people to whom hard pressed workers can go and off-load and relax, practical help with the families of youth workers. Without resources of people and money, these ministries cannot be sustained. Church facilities could be made available. Redundant and under-used plant can be adapted, but not if we insist on keeping it as it was. We can share ourselves and our young people. Who are to be the successors of those who have told their stories here? Where are those who like them are willing to give their lives to serve Christ amongst the least and the lost of our young people.

Faith in the City concludes:

'Our work as a Commission has put us in touch with some remarkable Church-sponsored youth work projects. A number of them are linked together and serviced by the Frontier Youth Trust. National organisations such as this can help those concerned with youth work (particularly in parishes) with advice and best practice. We believe that what has been done in some places can, with advice and support from such agencies, be done in others. We would like to record our gratitude for what we have seen, and recall the Church to its pioneering responsibility in the field of youth work' (*Faith in the City*, p. 323)

The task is global. Hard won experience in the UK is wanted by Christians in the exploding cities of Asia, Latin America and Africa. Mexico City expects to have 7 million young unemployed in a population of 31.5 million by the year 2000. These stories told with honesty and realism are pointers to others of what can be done here and now in the teeming cities of our globe. God challenges us to get involved, by being informed, praying, giving and offering the loaves and fishes of our lives for him to take and bless and break and share that multitudes may be fed.

Frontier Youth Trust

Frontier Youth Trust (FYT) is a network of Christian youth workers who are sharing Christ's love with disadvantaged young people.

Some work in open youth clubs, some in community centres, some in care units. Some work under the auspices of a local church or a denomination; others under the auspices of a local education authority or a national organisation or an independent board. Some are probation officers, some are social workers, some work with young people on the streets. Some are professionally trained; some are non-professional voluntary workers. All of them, as FYT members, affirm that Jesus is Lord of the whole of life.

The 'frontiers' where they work are our inner cities, large housing estates, areas of urban and rural deprivation. They're the toughest mission fields in Britain.

- *FYT provides youth workers in these tough situations with training, encouragement and pastoral care, and also with resources and with 'know how'.*

- *FYT has its own camping programmes.*

- *FYT stimulates local churches to reach out to young people in their communities.*

- *FYT also aims to act as an advocate to the rest of society – and in particular to Christians and to churches – on behalf of disadvantaged young people who feel voiceless and powerless.*

Frontier Youth Trust was founded in 1964, has been part of the Scripture Union Movement since 1966 and is celebrating its Silver Jubilee in 1989. For further information about FYT and details of ways in which you could support its work write to 130 City Road, London, EC1V 2NJ.